A Full Life
OR
the Life of a Fool

by

Richard L. Wilson

The contents of this work, including, but not limited to, the accuracy of events, people, and places depicted; opinions expressed; permission to use previously published materials included; and any advice given or actions advocated are solely the responsibility of the author, who assumes all liability for said work and indemnifies the publisher against any claims stemming from publication of the work.

All Rights Reserved
Copyright © 2021 by Richard L. Wilson

No part of this book may be reproduced or transmitted, downloaded, distributed, reverse engineered, or stored in or introduced into any information storage and retrieval system, in any form or by any means, including photocopying and recording, whether electronic or mechanical, now known or hereinafter invented without permission in writing from the publisher.

Dorrance Publishing Co
585 Alpha Drive
Pittsburgh, PA 15238
Visit our website at *www.dorrancebookstore.com*

ISBN: 978-1-6491-3835-4
eISBN: 978-1-6491-3996-2

To my mother Erma P. Wilson

My mother deserves a lot of credit for this book. She always stuck by us children in all ways a mother could. She was a peacemaker, a wonderful homemaker, a wonderful mother and a very hard worker. Even though only finishing 8th grade in her education, somehow she was able to spell nearly any word with ease. Even though she was never able to read this book, as she passed nearly a year ago, her presence is still here in our family. Thank you mom for all of your help in your life here on earth.

And thank you to Patti Parkes for her helping me arrange the book and pictures.

New Life:

The Early Years

On July 8, 1940, in the York Hospital, York, Pennsylvania, a child by the name of Richard Leroy Wilson was born to John Hyson Wilson and Erma Pearl Dellinger Wilson of Stewartstown, Pennsylvania. This child was born backwards, and that is just the beginning of what might be coming later. Does being born backwards, or breech as it is called by the medical profession, cause something different to the life involved in such an event, or was it just fate to keep the kid (meaning me) in the hospital along with his poor mom who was all torn up by this ordeal.

The York Hospital was not very big in 1940, and not many children were being born at that time. Very few were breech births as was my case. Because of this, my mom and I were not released until July 22, and during that time there in the baby ward something strange happened. A little girl named DeEtta Elaine Godfrey was born at that very same hospital, thus we know that she and I were together in that baby ward and who knows what might have gone on. Her parents were from Dallastown, Pennsylvania, some thirteen miles from where I was heading with my mom to join my dad. The Godfrey family did not know the Wilson family at that time, but because of fate or some other unknown reason, they would celebrate a wedding some nineteen years later between this pair of kids that may have already met for the first time in the baby ward of York Hospital.

John and Erma had made their temporary home outside of Stewartstown in a tenant house belonging to Russell Hersey. This house still stands near the Pleasant Valley Golf Course in East Hopewell Township. Erma, who grew up on the edge of Stewartstown, had quit school after eighth grade and gone to work at the sewing factory in Stewartstown. She gave her wages to her parents to help with the family's needs as there were ten children born to Harry and Gertrude Hersey Dellinger. This was a common thing for big families in those days. John Wilson was working for his neighbor Charles McCleary who owned a dairy farm. John's wages were $1 a day and two meals.

My mother, Erma, and myself at our first home after York Hospital; Russel Hersey tenant house in 1940.

Now in the next ten years, Erma would become a homemaker, wife, and mother of four children. At the time of this writing, Erma is one hundred years old. She is still sharp as a tack and just gave up driving at the age of ninety-eight.

A Full Life or Life of a Fool

The tenant house, where the new Wilson family of now three lived until November of 1940, was actually owned by Erma's Uncle Russell Hersey and was the brother of her mother Gertrude Hersey Dellinger. Most all of these small farms in this area had a tenant house on them for someone to live there and work on the farm. This one was empty at the time and rented by the new Wilson family. John had grown up just across the field on his family farm of many years. John's family consisted of three sisters, one brother, and his mother Imo Bartol Wilson and his father Charles Alexander Wilson.

By this time, now 1940–1941, my great grandmother had moved into a new home on North Main Street in Stewartstown, some two and a half miles from the farm. I never saw my great grandfather, but I remember seeing my great grandmother Emma only once. Because of the dislike my grandmother had for her mother-in-law, they kept apart. I never knew the details, but I believe I would have liked my great grandmother because of all that I have learned about her in more recent years at our family reunions. She was apparently a lot of fun and that was what Grandma Imo seemed to not like. I have never been able to understand that side of her, but it was very clearly present as part of her personality.

Knowing that if they were going to raise a family, which was their plan and desire, John and Erma with their new son Richard, which I was called for forty-five years, decided that they would try to buy a farm and put their dream into action. John heard about a farm located in Fawn Township, some seven or eight miles to the south, near the edge of the village of Gatchellville. This farm was for sale because the Eddie family estate had to be settled, and Mr. Ross Anderson was the executor. Mr. Anderson was a machinery dealer in New Park, and John bought the farm and some equipment from Mr. Anderson. John purchased a Farmall H tractor with steel wheels, as the war was still causing a shortage of rubber. So the rubber tires came later. Also purchased was a horse-drawn corn planter, cultivators, and a New Idea manure spreader. Mr. Anderson generously gave Dad a new spring-tooth harrow to go along with the other equipment. My dad always spoke highly of Mr. Anderson, and three generations later our families have many happy relationships and memories to look back upon.

John also bought a couple of horses for the farming operation. A red horse named Scotty and a black and white horse named Prince. The horse dealer did not want to give the horses on credit to my dad, and this is how the story goes. Harry Dellinger, my grandpa and Erma's father, knew the horse dealer. He told my dad to go back to him and tell him that Harry Dellinger said that if he would not sell the horses to my dad on credit to "stick them up your ass!" Somehow, someway, this statement caused the horse dealer to sell them on credit to my dad. Harry Dellinger was known to have a quick temper and could get stirred up rather quickly. But his word was respected in the community, and during the 1940s that often times meant the difference in what did or did not happen.

The two horses that my dad bought in 1942, Scotty and Prince.

My grandpa Harry was a painter by trade and a small time farmer who raised chickens and sold their eggs. He and Grandma Gertrude had raised ten children, and my mother Erma was next to the youngest. I remember visiting that small farm as a young lad and being amazed at the big stacks of Zane Grey western novels that my grandpa had by his chair in the corner by the stove. All these seemingly small details play an important part in what happens in the future of this journey.

The purchase of this farm in rural Fawn Township was comprised of approximately 185 acres of ground and cost $5,500.00. About 85 acres were tillable ground at the time of purchase. Some of the ground was very steep and erosion had removed a lot of the topsoil in many places. While about 50 acres were prime farm ground, there was also much wooded land. At the time, it was good enough to get started, and that was the big push for my dad.

Later on in the early 1960s, the family discovered that the wooded ground was prime for wildlife and especially for the white-tailed deer. To this very day, many of the family members enjoy hunting on this farm and appreciate the years of great fun and fellowship that the deer hunting season has brought their way. The gals would always provide a big lunch for the hunters and we would sit and tell stories of the fun we had that morning and then head back to the woods for whatever was left of the day. Even though our family is no longer engaged in the actual farming of the land, we still own the majority of the farm and woods. While a grandson does the farming, we all continue to hunt on the land. Our family has remained close, and my siblings and I have a partnership that takes care of the ground that is left as well as some other property.

In 1940 there was a tenant house on the farm, and John Wilson hired a black man named John Giles to work for him on the farm. Mr. Giles along with his wife, Lucy, and several of their children lived in the tenant house. It sat across the field and was near the extra barn or tobacco shed. There was a stream that ran through the center of the farm, and it dumped its water into a larger stream that ran across the northern part of the farm.

Winter snows at the farm with my dad John H. Wilson.

The farmhouse in which we lived had about a 500-foot long lane off of the road running to the small community of Gatchellville, which was one-mile south of our home. The house was not large: three bedrooms, an attic, a bathroom, a small hallway, a large living room, a dining room, a small kitchen and a pantry. A front porch and back porch had stairs that led down to ground level. There was also an inside stairway that led to the basement part of the house which was a ground cellar for a long time and a small cellar we called the egg cellar. We heated the house with wood and coal until the 1950s when we changed over to a water heater system that was fed with coal and later heating oil. A large black tank made of steel was used as a pressure tank but had to be removed in the 1960s. It was very old, and I used a torch that I then had on the farm to cut it up into pieces. While doing this, a very large splat of red hot molten steel from the tank got into my work shoe through one of the lace keeper holes and burned its way deep into my foot. I carry that scar to this very day.

Outside of the egg cellar was a large wooden top that sat over a hand dug well that had been used for water in previous years. That top which looked like a large table was about 12 by 12 feet and sat about 3 feet high. We never used that well, but there are some stories about it that always amazed me. Old Mr. Eddie who had owned the farm had dug the well himself. He would take dynamite into the hole as he dug it, and when it got too deep for him to climb out, he would light the dynamite and give the mule instructions to pull him out. The well was over 55 feet deep, and I guess the old faithful mule never failed to pull Mr. Eddie out. Sometime during the '60s or '70s the wooden top was removed, and a cement cap was put in place of the wooden one.

Across from the house was a small brooder house used to raise baby chicks which were bought from the hatchery in the spring. They were raised to lay eggs to sell in order to help pay the bills. A one-car garage was alongside of that to house the car. On the other side of the brooder house was a large shed with attached corn cribs which were used for machinery storage and repair work. A very large barn sat not far away which was used to store hay, straw, and other crops used to feed the animals and chicken that were housed in the bottom of that barn and in the chicken house adjacent to the barn.

Across the field and near the tenant house was a medium-size barn that had been used for tobacco storage before 1940. This structure would be used for storing potatoes after the Wilson family took over. This building was located on a dirt road now called West Maple Lawn Road and was connected to the main road that ran from our farm to Gatchellville which was one mile away. Then it went on to New Park for three miles. If you turned left on that road at the top of our lane you would end up in Muddy Creek Forks in three miles. John Wilson and his hired man John Giles worked this farm, and I can remember several things that happened that are worth mentioning.

I did not get to see much of the farm until I was a few years older. In 1942, my sister Glenda was born. Of course, Mom was busy with cooking and taking care of my sister. I think I was also busy doing things that caused my mom extra work and worry. I do not remember this, but I was told that I upset my baby sister's crib onto the heater grate. I also tried to get the bottom plate out of the cabinet in the kitchen instead of taking the top plate and wound up breaking the entire stack which was all we had at the time. I believe I caused a lot of trouble for my parents as a youngster, and I feel bad that all that happened; but I am so grateful that they loved me enough to continue to raise me and tried to direct me in the right direction. They must have believed and trusted that someday it would be worthwhile. I am still not sure if being born backwards was part of the cause or if I was just a kid with a chip on my shoulder and destined to go through some tough times, perhaps as punishment for my temper and my sometimes nasty disposition.

My dad had a wagon bed built to put on a set of running gears that he had found somewhere. We used that wagon to haul big cedar trees that we would cut down on the northern part of the farm. We would put these large trees in these deep gutters with the top of the tree facing up hill. Some of these gutters were more than six feet deep, and some were wider than three feet. The limbs would catch the silt from the flooding thunderstorms in the summer and then start to fill the gutter. Looking at those fields today, it is hard to imagine that gutters like that existed there in the early 1940s. Later on we cleared that large area of cedar trees and turned it into productive farming ground.

On one occasion when John Giles was in the back part of the farm, Dad sent him off to the house driving the H tractor which John did not want to do. Dad told Mr. Giles to head for the barn which was about ½ mile away. He told him that he would be there in time to stop the tractor at the open barn doors. For some reason, Dad was a bit delayed in getting to the barn. Mr. Giles had already entered the barn and would soon reach the part of the barn that would not bear the weight of the tractor. John was just following the instructions that Dad had given to him. Just in the nick of time, Dad got the tractor stopped preventing what could have been a very bad accident. I do know for a fact that Mr. Giles was never on that tractor again!

It was soon evident that my dad was to become a potato farmer, potatoes being a common crop to grow in our area. However, this would require more machinery to be purchased and our crop rotation was to be potatoes, followed by wheat, and then back into potatoes. This we did on our better ground, leaving the other acres for corn, wheat, and then clover hay to be grown. We also had a few steers, a couple of cows, and some pigs and chickens.

Now, John Wilson had a green thumb, and this simply meant he really understood how to raise a crop like potatoes that required more knowledge and skill than raising corn, wheat, and hay. John's father, my grandfather Charles, was already raising potatoes, cabbage, tomatoes, and other vegetables. Grandpa had a small Chevy truck, and he made a trip to York (located about 25 miles north) each week on a certain day and delivered beautiful produce to several store keepers in the city.

My great grandparents, Mr. & Mrs. John A. Wilson, who built the Wilson home in 1891. Pictured with their two sons, Charles (my grandfather) is the older and Harry, the younger.

Grandpa was also one of the three original board members of the newly formed York County Potato Growers Association. In the 1940s York County, Pennsylvania, was one of the leading potato producing areas in the state. The climate was overall very compatible for growing potatoes, and the soil was well drained. In later years, both my dad and I served on the board of directors of this organization. However, because things happen to change what goes on where in agriculture, that organization is not even in existence today because there are virtually no potatoes grown in York County anymore.

By 1955 or 1957, there were seven active potato chip plants within York County or just over the line into two other counties-all within 50–60 miles of each other. Thus, the potato business was huge in York County which caused those farmers raising potatoes to do very well because of the proximity of the markets that purchased their produce. York County still has these factories to make potato chips and snacks, but all the raw materials, mostly potatoes, are shipped in from the upper Midwest and other areas. I will explain later what caused this unbelievable change. Its effects were wide-spread in our area and were somewhat of a big discouragement to all those that it affected, and that was every potato farmer within miles of where we lived.

The old Wilson Homestead during the summer; threshing machine is steam powered.

As I loved to be with my dad on the farm, I always tagged along as close to him as I could. I can remember sneaking out of the house, probably age four, to try to get close to what was going on. By the time I was five years old, our neighbor Frank McCleary put me up on his big M Farmall tractor during wheat harvest and told me to steer the tractor between the wheat sheaves that were placed on the ground by the binder that had tied those sheaves.

This was one of the biggest thrills of my young life, and Mr. McCleary would jump on the draw bar of the tractor, reach up, and push the clutch when he wanted me to stop. Several men, including my dad, were loading the sheaves onto the wagon, and when loaded, Mr. McCleary would drive it into the barn. My little short legs did not reach the clutch or brake from the seat, but the ground was level, and I was able to help do farm work, and I loved every second of that. Had my mother known what was going on out in that field, it would not have been good, and I was smart enough to know that and kept it quiet for some time to come. I was a fairly big kid for my age and strong and was allowed to help more and more as time went by. There was no TV then and nothing to do in the house that interested me.

In February, we would get our Certified Seed Potatoes from the state of Maine and put them in the potato cellar by the tenant house. The men had a cutting box that the potatoes were dumped into, and they would sit by this big box that held perhaps 300 pounds of seed potatoes. With a big paring knife with the blade sticking up through the wood frame, they would pull or push the seed potato through, trying to get at least one eye in each seed piece that was to be planted into the ground. If the seed piece did not have a good eye in it, there would be no sprout and no potato plant, so naturally, the goal was to make sure of at least one good eye in each seed piece. By March of 1946, I was in the potato cellar helping the men to cut potatoes. My job was to cut open the strings that held the bags closed and to dump the potatoes into the big cutting box so that my dad and Mr. Giles could keep cutting. Sometimes my mom would also help do the task of cutting up the seed into good seed pieces with a good eye. Even though I could not pick up these 100 pound bags of certified seed potatoes, I was still able to tilt the bag into a smaller basket and carry about 25 pounds at a time and dump it into the big box. As I dumped the last potatoes out of a bag, I would neatly put the empty bag on a pile so that we could use the bags later on for the harvest. I was amazed as I opened the bags because there were several tags on each bag, and the name and address

A Full Life or Life of a Fool

of the grower in Maine or Prince Edward Island would be on the bag. This interested me because one summer my family and I took a trip to the area in northern Maine from where this seed came.

Believe me when I say it took a lot of time to do this job. This had to be done before planting, and planting started in mid to late March or early April. Some of the little secrets were to warm up the potato cellar so the potatoes were starting to sprout by the time that they were planted. They would come out of the ground quicker when this was done, and we used to dip the freshly cut potatoes in a solution of Captan to help preserve the seed piece from rotting before they sprouted.

One nice day in mid to late April, perhaps in 1947, we were just about to finish up cutting seed. Dad had said that if we could finish up by lunch we would be all done, and, of course, that was the goal. It was warm outside, and we had the potato cellar doors wide open to let in the good warm spring air. We were running a bit late, but we were hopeful to get it done by 12:15 or 12:20. About 12:10, a loud voice could be heard up on the hill from the tenant house, and it was Mrs. Giles, the wife of John, who was there cutting potatoes with my dad. Lucy, as she was called, yelled loudly, and she was a big woman with a loud voice. She was about 100 yards away and screamed loudly. "Don't you know it is dinner time?" A moment of silence, and then her husband John yelled louder than I had ever heard him yell, "God damn it; if you are hungry, EAT!" My dad chuckled a bit and was still chuckling as we went up to our house to eat around 12:30.

Potatoes were a crop that kept us busy for most of the year. Later in the '50s as the seed came in by February, we then prepared it for planting in March and April. By May we were hoeing them or cultivating them and spraying them for insects and blight. We irrigated during July and August. In late August, we started harvesting them and that lasted until early October. By late October, we finished packing the cellar full so that we could grade out and sell to neighbors, stores, and schools until they were all gone, and then we would start over again.

My last memory of Mr. Giles was several years later as he was dying with cancer in the tenant house and asked for my dad to come over. I begged Dad to go along. Somehow I believed that I would never see him again if I did not go with my dad that day. I was permitted to go with him. As he lay there dying, and was covered with flies, he apologized to my dad for not paying the rent which was included in his salary. As he was unable to work, he knew the rent was not being paid, and he felt bad and wanted to keep straight with my dad. My dad said, "John, you do not owe me anything, and this is your home as long as you live." He died shortly after that, and his wife Lucy moved away at some later date. I was so proud of my dad for the way he handled that, and I knew he was a good man. I also remember a year before that when dad took Mr. Giles along to Baltimore with a load of potatoes. They were coming home through Towson and stopped at a White Coffee Pot Restaurant. As they sat down to order, the manager came back and said that Mr. Giles would have to stand in the rear, and that he could not sit to eat. My dad told him that if he could not sit then they would leave. So they came home hungry. Mr. Giles remarked on the way back to the truck, "I do not know what is wrong with these sons of bitches down here. We just live 45 miles north, and we do not have those kind of problems in our community." We lived about three or four miles north of the Mason Dixon Line.

My grandpa weighing potatoes during the late 1950's.

When Mr. Giles passed away, the horses were sold. Our farming operation was evolving. Because of no horses, we needed to buy more and different machinery. Along with that change came my brother Ronald who was born in March of 1946. Now my mother had more extra work to do. More clothes to wash and iron, more food to prepare, more chores to do; occasionally, some extra help would arrive to aid my mom. By now we were a family of five and still growing.

At this time, we had a more modern two row potato planter, and the H Farmall struggled to pull it up some of the hills. We had a potato sprayer that replaced the custom sprayer that used to come to our farm and do that chore. We had a 1947 Chevy truck that was used to haul the potatoes to market.

One day while we were planting potatoes and the H Farmall was struggling a bit pulling the planter up some of the hills, a machinery salesman stopped by and tried to sell dad a big M Farmall. That was a bigger tractor and would have handled the potato planter with more ease. The salesman was Donald Keesey and was distantly related to our family. Dad got a little ticked off at his high pressure tactics, and after Mr. Keesey said that Dad needed a big M, Dad shot back at him with, "What I need is a million dollars!" The salesman took the hint and left the farm quickly. Mr. Keesey later became an industrial arts teacher at the soon to come Kennard Dale High School.

At this time, I was ready to start grade one in our local school. The school bus was to pick me up at the head of our lane. We had a big hickory tree to sort of get behind to be protected from the wind chill in the colder months while waiting on the bus. Starting school was to be a very mixed bag for me because at the age of two years it was detected that I was very cross-eyed. I had been taken to a Dr. Bruce Grove in York, Pennsylvania. Very soon I was wearing eye glasses, not normal for a two-year-old, and worse than that, I had to wear a black rubber stopper over my left eye to try to strengthen the muscle in my right eye. That is all they knew to do at the time. Now, a simple operation to cut the weaker eye muscle and move the eye and reattach it is the direction taken. Wearing glasses was not a real big issue until I started to go to school.

It started with getting on the bus and the kids calling me "four eyes" and "freak." They would point at me and make fun of me. My temper, that was most likely present in my body and mind, often responded at these times. Older kids would tease me too, and when I went to hit them to make them stop, they would hold me away from them because my shorter arms could not hurt them as I swung and swung. Kids can be really cruel, and I dealt with this and other problems caused by my very crossed eyes. Not until I got into the Marine Corps was I simply forced to deal with this physical problem that life had dealt me. Of course, I had a circle of friends that made it more tolerable for me, and I survived. But wearing glasses was a pain for me, and the wearing of a patch on the left eye made it even more noticeable to the public.

At this time in my life the local church of Prospect Methodist, located at the edge of Gatchellville, became a big part of my young life. There was Children's Day, Christmas programs, and Memorial Day Strawberry and Ice Cream. On one occasion, my father had to come up and retrieve me from a fist fight in the choir loft while one of these programs was going on. Some kid was teasing me because of my crossed eyes and my temper got me into trouble. My eyes were a mess, but I could not do anything to help that. Church was usually a fun place to be, and I enjoyed learning the Bible stories that I am sure helped to shape my coming years.

On the farm, we were about to expand our poultry operation and had hired a couple of neighbors to build a new brooder house to raise little chicks since the one across the road from the farm was too small. We also bought three brooder houses from Bill Fergurson, an elderly neighbor, as he was quitting the chicken business. Ralph McCleary, another neighbor, who was very handy and could build or fix anything, tore down an old silo that stood unused by the barn that was being changed into a large chicken house. Now half of that large barn would house well over a 1,000 laying hens.

Our old farmhouse had a good slate roof on it, but when it snowed and blew, the fine snow would come into the attic. Dad would always go up with a broom, shovel, and a bucket and gather it up before it melted and came down through the house. Dad did this for 60-plus years until he fell down the attic steps. After that, I put plastic in the attic so that what snow did come in would just melt and evaporate away.

Down in our basement, which was divided into two parts, there was a ground cellar with a coal bin in the back corner and a smaller room with a cement floor used for packing and cleaning eggs.

Each year we would kill three to five pigs weighing over 250 pounds each to provide our pork needs for the year. We would take them to the custom butcher some 6 miles away, and he would cut up the meat and do some processing of the meat. Then we would pick it up and bring it home. Included were some pudding meat, scrapple, tenderloins, lard, and best of all, the shoulders and hams. In the basement, Dad would build a large makeshift table each year out of wooden planks and put the hams and shoulders on that table. He then made a mixture of brown sugar, salt peter, pepper, and not sure what else, and would rub that into the outside of the large hams and shoulders. He would turn them every few days and repeat that process for perhaps a month. Then he would put them in a tight bag and hang them on meat hooks in a small building out back called a smokehouse. He would smoke them for a long time using green wood. After that process was completed, they would just hang there until spring when we would start to eat them. That meat was so good, and when my mom's brothers would come down on a Sunday afternoon, we got to enjoy a delicious meal.

Around 4 p.m., one of my aunts would say, "Walter or Emory, we must go home." My mom would then reply, "Why don't you stay for supper? Then one of my aunts would say, "No, that is too much work for you." Walter or Emory would then say, "What are you having?" Mom would reply, "Country ham and fried potatoes." I was cheering in the background because I wanted to have some of that good ham, and no matter what, mom's brother would say, "WE ARE STAYING!" Then Dad would go to the smoke house and get down a ham because they were the best. The hams were saved for special occasions and special company. Dad would remove the ham from the sack, and then he would trim off the outside which was that special rub recipe. Even that old cure being trimmed away smelled good enough to eat. Dad would use a meat saw to cut through the ham bone and carefully prepare nice slices of ham for Mom to fry. That saw had special teeth and was never used for anything else except to cut meat. I would snitch a small piece of raw ham and chew on it as dad was carving up the ham for Mom.

Our house had a big living room, and the far end was plusher and very nice. That was where the women would sit to visit. There were many happy times in that house with the aunts, uncles, and cousins.

New Life 2:

The Pre-Teen Years

My first paid for haircut was in the Fawn Grove Barber Shop. I am not sure at what age, but I screamed so loudly that many folks thought someone had been hurt! The only thing that was hurt were my feelings and, most likely, my dad's patience.

Some years later in the same barber shop, some farmer by the name of Warren Wallace, who had a reputation of pulling pranks on kids, asked me if I had a pony. I told him no. He asked me if I would like to have one, and I said yes. He told me that he would see that I got one, and I was excited. My dad told me that he would never get me one, and he did this to kids. I still wanted to believe him, but Dad was right. No pony!

At the age of five, I was very interested in farming. So much so, that when my mom planted a garden, I took a lima bean seed and stuck it up my nose to see what would happen. Nothing happened, but I could not get it out. So being my normal born-backwards self, I just forgot about it. Two days later when my nose began to swell up and they had to rush me to a doctor in York, I had to "spill the beans!" They put an ether tent on me to put me to sleep so they could extract the bean from its spot. It took four people to hold me down, but the ether finally took hold. The next thing I knew was that I had a thermometer in my mouth, and I promptly bit it in half! Now they were worried that I had swallowed mercury out of the thermometer.

My sister Glenda and I in 1945.

We had this really nice black English Shepherd dog that was named Shep. He would go down and bring up the cows from the meadow if they did not appear at milking time. We loved that dog a lot. I remember one day while Dad was spraying the clover hay with a pesticide called Heptachlor which was used to kill spittle bugs, that Shep followed Dad all day and Shep was soaked to his skin. He smelled of Heptachlor all summer long, but he never had a tick on him all year long which was unusual for a farm dog.

Shep had one very bad habit and that was chasing vehicles. We tried to break him, but he just could not stand seeing a car or truck without giving chase. One morning while we were down at the potato cellar, a truck from the neighbor's farm came by. The problem was that it was a tractor and a trailer with an extra axle. Shep got run over and died later that day. There were many tears that day, and we all missed him.

Going to school at Fawn Grove Elementary in a class of about 30 kids was a new experience. Wearing glasses was a pain, and it seemed like I was destined to break my glasses. That always meant a trip to York and more expense for my parents. This school was small and only had first and second grades. I will never be able to tell why I did this, but for some reason I kissed a girl who was in the second grade, and I was reported to the substitute teacher. She immediately came to the far part of the playground where I was. She got me by the ear and took me some 200 yards to the classroom. One thing that I clearly learned was that when someone got a kid by the ear, that person got total control of him. My nose was not more than a foot from the ground the whole 200 yards. Just for the record, the father of that girl later offered me my first job.

Third grade found us with an often-time substitute teacher, Daisy Brown. I will always remember that she taught us Roman numerals in math. I always thought that was kind of neat, and I never forgot those letters that were numbers. Also, the teacher's desk was so big and Mrs. Brown was so short that you could barely see her when she sat at the desk. One day she was provoked about kids being out of their seats. So she set a mouse trap in front of her desk and declared that we would be caught if we got out of our seats. A kid that was a good friend of mine, and still is, crawled up and pushed the trap up near Mrs. Brown's feet. He then retreated to his seat without being caught because she was unable to see him. Shortly thereafter, she set off the trap with her foot and nearly upset her desk in astonishment. Unless someone told her later, I do not think she ever figured it out. There was also a kid in our third grade (the year was 1949) who chewed tobacco! When he would sneeze, he spread tobacco juice over several of the girls' papers who sat near him.

Fourth grade found me in Miss McElwain's class. She was very strict, kept order, and was a good math teacher. Just for the record, she was the first person to sign a petition for me to run for school director in Southeastern School District some forty years later.

My fifth grade teacher was Mrs. McDonald who had recently married my future neighbor and dear friend Wiest McDonald. They were both older when married for the first time. Edith, later in life, told me that the worst mistake she ever made in teaching was in our class. A red-headed student whom some called "cesspool" and sat in the front row, had left a very smelly fart. She was teaching English and had just explained the difference of how to say the flowers smelled sweetly. Her example was, "Flowers don't smell; I smell." All of a sudden, bang, there came the odor. She paused and very clearly asked, "Does anyone in here have to go to the restroom?" The kid seated behind the guilty party said, "What about you, Cess?" He jumped up and hit the kid and took off out of the room.

Our sixth grade teacher was Mrs. Hess who was also a good math teacher. She had a son in the class ahead of ours who would later become a state senator in the Pennsylvania legislature. One day a Mr. Bobby Brown came to our school and dropped off several basketballs, which was the beginning of a new experience for us. Later that year, we had tryouts in foul shooting down at the community hall in Fawn Grove. That is where the local team the Fawn Grove RED Skins played in a county league. They were pretty good, and I enjoyed going with my father where we would get close to the coal stove to keep warm while we watched. My Uncle Howard Burkins was a referee, and he told me that he had to quit because he could not sleep at night after the games as he replayed them while trying to sleep. I knew that the next part of my education would be in the new consolidated school just on the north edge of Fawn Grove. This school was to be called Kennard Dale.

When my sister Glenda started to school in 1948, we both got on the school bus together at the end of our farm lane. Sometime, perhaps in 1950, my sister and I got the idea that if we would walk up to the service station on the corner of our farm, that we could be with other kids there waiting for the bus. We were hopeful that we could spend a penny there in the store and get two pieces of candy for one cent which was the price at that time. Since I contrived the idea, I asked Mr. Marshall Wilson (no relation), if we could do that. He said yes, so my way of telling my dad was to say that Marshall Wilson would like us to get on the bus at the service station from that time on. The next day was the only day that our dad walked with us up the lane to the bus stop. When the bus stopped, my dad asked Marshall Wilson where the kids were to get on the bus. Mr. Marshall calmly replied, "Right here." So no more was said about that. My big plans had failed.

The next big event in the family was the arrival of our baby sister Gloria in 1950. Now there were six Wilsons in the completed family. My mom had some help at child birth, and this lady made some spinach for us for supper. We had been taught to clean up our plates. Mom was a great cook, but as I looked down at the prepared or not prepared spinach with no dressing, I knew this was bad. I glanced up at Dad, and the most wonderful thing happened. He gently shook his head no, and I read that loud and clear. What a relief!

A Full Life or Life of a Fool

We grew up across the field from the McCleary family and were very close to them as we churched together and sometimes went on vacations together. Two other friends were Mr. and Mrs. Ollie Martin who owned the service station at the southeast corner of our property. Their grandson spent a lot of time with them in the summer months. This boy was a lot of fun, and he brought along a ball that would not bounce right. He said it was a football. I questioned how it could be a ball, and he explained all that to me. He always had a bunch of baseball and football cards with him. He would hand them to me so that I would ask him questions about the statistics on the cards. He knew everything that was on them. I was always amazed. He would later go to a neighboring school about twenty miles west of Kennard Dale. For several years, he helped pick up potatoes in late August before school started. We spent many hours playing together, and then he was gone. I never saw him again until I thought I saw him on TV during an Oakland Raiders Super Bowl game. At that time, I lived near his aunt. She explained that it was him, as he was the head scout for the Oakland Raiders! He later became the general manager of the Green Bay Packers and was inducted into the Football Hall of Fame in 2015.

One morning when I was just ten years old, I awoke, and as I went into the bathroom I saw my father shaving and I thought he was sobbing. I asked him what was going on, and he told me that my Grandpa Dellinger had passed away. This was the first death in the family that I had experienced. I was shocked to see my dad in tears. Grandpa had had a heart attack, and Mom had already left to go up to her home. Grandpa Harry had stacks of Zane Grey books, almost as tall as me, in the basement of their house. They had ten kids so they needed all the upstairs area for their sleeping quarters. The down- stairs where they lived had a ceiling of only about 6 1/2 feet. There was a ground cellar which was dark and cool in which to keep the eggs in from the chicken house. My Grandma Dellinger used to love to play dominoes with her brother Chester Hersey, I would watch in amazement as a youngster as they moved the ivory pieces around hearing them click as they touched one another.

My other grandparents lived most of their lives on the farm in East Hopewell Township about 2 ½ miles from Stewartstown and about eight miles from our farm in Fawn Township. I spent a good deal of time at my grandparents' farm. Sometimes I would stay for a week during the summer. Grandpa Wilson had a great sense of humor while my grandma could be very sour. She seemed to think that having fun was wrong. I used to love to go with grandpa on his truck produce route to York. His customers loved to see him as he always had lovely produce to offer them at their city stores. On the way home, we would stop at an ice cream store between Spry and Dallastown. It was called Mack's Ice Cream. They made their own and it was so good. You could get a twenty-cent plate, and it was so much because the dips were so big. Sometimes Grandpa would buy a two or two-and-a-half gallon container and take it home. The Macks had a big family, and one time when they got to the bottom of an ice cream container, there was a dirty diaper in the bottom! No law suit then—just a free container of ice cream and a good story for the ages.

Grandpa used to throw stones at a stray tom cat and yell, "Thomas Stinker!" I learned that a tom cat's pee both stinks and stings as it enters the eyes because one day as I jumped up in the shed and grabbed the tail of a tom cat, he pissed in my eyes and it hit the bridge of my nose and split off into my eyes.

Grandpa Wilson served on the school board as secretary and kept the school supplies in one of the many rooms of his huge house. There were many books there, and I sometimes would entertain myself as I visited. That house was so big that it was fun to just walk through it and look at the many rooms. One day as I found an old school bell out back by the ice house, I set it up and made it ding dong for several minutes. Neighbors started rolling in because that was the sign of an emergency. I did not know that but certainly found it out quickly. That was the one time I remember my grandpa being very angry with me. Grandpa Wilson was also treasurer of the Round Hill Presbyterian Church. He kept a big safe with a combination lock on it. I used to watch him in amazement as he opened it. I later bought it a sale, and it is in a safe place for another generation to have. His name is on the safe, and I was always impressed.

Grandma had two sides to her personality. She could be and was very kind to neighbors and children as she held a Bible club in her house on Sunday afternoons for children in the neighborhood. Some of these kids walked several miles to grandma's house. She would tell Bible stories using flannel graph. She served sandwiches and ice cream afterwards. That was enough to get a lot of kids involved with nothing better to do. It would be hard to measure the success that she may have had on children of that neighborhood, but no one could say that she did not try to help the children.

One incident that I will never forget was during one of these Bible club meetings. After the meeting, I sat on the swing on the huge porch. There was a young gal, perhaps three or so years older than me, who I had never seen before. She sat down beside me and kissed me! I did not even know her name, but it was kind of nice. This aroused a part of me that I had never noticed before. Even at the tender age of eleven, I knew that was something special. Yet, I never knew her name but would not forget that experience as long as I live. As fate would have it some forty years later, as I purchased some lumber at the Lumber Yard in Stewartstown for a project I was working on, I wrote out a check. This clerk took it and looked at it. She looked at me, and I knew that this was the girl on the swing at Grandma's house that day. She knew also and asked me if I was related to Imo Wilson. I told her I was and that I was the boy on the swing. We laughed, and I suddenly realized that her step-brother had worked for me. I had never put that all together until that day. This lady had lost her husband in a tragic truck accident just a few months earlier. He was returning a trailer to Lancaster County that he had used to move he and his wife from Montana back to the Stewartstown area.

Grandma was not a really happy person. It was always hard for me to understand how she could be so religious and helpful and yet be so seemingly unhappy. As a child my thoughts about this just came and went, but as I grew older I began to realize that she was estranged from my grandpa's mother, Emma. Because of that, even though Emma lived in Stewartstown, I never ever got to see her. All reports were that she was a lovely, happy person, full of fun. I always felt I missed something good by never getting to know her. Things that were often amusing to others seemed to be a near sin to my grandma.

It seemed like we were getting along pretty well on the farm as we had bought a new car and truck in 1947. We were adding equipment to the farming operation. We bought a new 1950 Ford 8N tractor with rear cultivators and a weeder. This tractor had a three- point hitch which made it quicker to hook up the implements. We had Ferd Webb, an experienced welder and garage owner, to come to the farm and adapt the horse drawn corn planter to that tractor, along with several other things to make it easier to make time in the farming operation. A new Oliver potato digger laid the potatoes out very nicely as it seemed to separate the ground and rocks from the potatoes and made them easier to pick up from the ground.

At that time, we would put two 5/8th bushel baskets of potatoes in a 100-pound burlap sack which was usually around 70–75 pounds. We then loaded them on a wagon and hauled them out of the field to the truck where we loaded them. Dad would haul them to the UTZ potato chip plant in Hanover and even return with another load on some days-always one load, but sometimes two. This made me very busy as I was going to school and working until 11:00 P.M. out in the fields. Mom would be out driving the tractor for us and would have a snack before bed as we finished up for the day. We had several men work for us during that time, and one was Roman Spahr, who lived in the tenant house.

One of the best workers we ever had working for us was a black lady named Bertha James. She could pick 200 bags a day and was such a nice lady. Dad would sometimes hire her to help mom out. She could iron a white shirt better and faster than anyone I had ever seen. I loved to watch her kill chicken roosters that we were going to eat. Dad used to cut off their heads, and this lady just got hold of their necks and snapped off their heads in such a way as to not lose any meat from the neck. She was married to a guy named Red James and they lived near Muddy Creek Forks. She was the most wonderful lady, and I loved her dearly and just enjoyed being around her. Fate would have it that her husband got drunk and shot her. She lost her eyesight and disappeared from our lives forever.

New Life 3:

Almost Old Enough to Drive

One day as my dad was getting ready to milk the cow, I got the bright idea to climb into the old horse trough that was no longer in use. This trough was part of the stall where the horses were chained when not working. It was not used any more after the horses were all sold. My plan was to wait until dad came in with the cow who was down in the meadow. As dad chained her to her regular stall some ten yards from where I was hiding in the horse trough, I imitated an old tom cat as I forced out a big meow, really trying to sound like a real cat. I was not sure my dad had heard me, and I knew that he would go to the house to get the milk bucket. So I just relaxed and waited for his return. My dad hated old stray tom cats and was not past putting them through whatever punishment that he could. There was about a two inch round hole in the top of the trough in which I was lying, and I could look out that hole without being seen by my dad. Dad did not return for about five minutes, so I continued to relax and did not pay much attention. I knew that he would make enough noise on his return to the stable that I would hear him. Then I would meow again. I was now amusing myself with this stunt that I had concocted and thinking how neat it was "to get one over" on my dad.

All of a sudden as I began to once again look out the hole in the trough, I was shocked to see my father approaching the trough. Dad was creeping quietly. What was really bad was that he did not have the milk bucket in his hand, but rather he held the twenty-two rifle that was kept in the pantry near the milk bucket. When I first saw him about twelve feet away, I was so shocked that I could not holler or say anything. But by the time he was about six feet away, I eased out a very gentle, "Dad, I am in the trough; please don't shoot." That was a scary moment for both my dad and myself. Yet we were able to laugh about it at supper time as the story was told to my mom and the rest of the Wilson family.

My brother Ronald and my sister Gloria in 1957.

We were busy planting several varieties of potatoes. The Irish Cobbler was planted and harvested because it was a short season variety. The Kennebec was mainly used for potato chips however people loved them because they made exceptionally good French fries. The Katahdin was a full season potato and good for keeping in storage until late winter. It was a very easy potato to pack and take to the fresh market. It was very smooth skinned and had a nice shape and just looked good to the consumer. A few years later for one of my FFA projects, I planted one acre of Russet Rural. This variety was especially good for potato chips.

I used to watch the blue tags on the certified seed that we bought to see the name of the grower. Most of the seed was from Maine, but sometimes it came from Prince Edward Island. Around this time, we took a trip to Maine

A Full Life or Life of a Fool

to see the potatoes being grown, mostly in Aroostook County way up in northern Maine next to Canada. We saw big beautiful fields of red clover along with the many acres of potatoes. This was a vacation that we took in two different cars. Both were Chevy's. One belonged to the McCleary family who lived across the field from us, and the other belonged to the Wilson family. We took several vacations this way, following one another and stopping to stay in some rural motel or group of cottages that offered a good price—but nothing fancy.

During the summer months, we would make hay, and since we no longer had horses, we had to do things a little differently now. The hay was put in loose and loaded into the wagon with a New Idea (a brand of machinery) hay loader. Every big barns like ours had a hay fork and a track in the peak of the barn. The hay fork would be hooked to the new Ford 8N tractor, and I was allowed to run that tractor which would pull up huge piles of loose hay from the wagon. When they were ready for me to move forward, I was given a signal. Slowly, I would proceed forward towards the gas pump which was some forty yards ahead. When they yelled again, I would stop and back up. That would allow the person on the wagon to pull the hay fork which dumped the big wad of hay. Then with that small rope he would pull the big fork back down to the wagon while several men would be spreading the hay with pitch forks in the mow in order to keep it even.

I was always trying to break the record as to how far I could go before they yelled to stop. That was really not too smart because if I ever went too far, it would have busted something up in the top of the barn. This hay was used to feed the livestock in the winter when there was no grass in the pasture. It was hard work digging it out and throwing it down the hay hole at the corner of the hay mow which was about thirty by forty feet. It got to be about twenty to twenty-five feet deep as the haying season ended.

Prospect Methodist, our local church, was situated on the edge of Gatchellville. It was a big part of our young lives and our family as we attended services most every week on Sunday morning and during some special services and events that were held there. On Memorial Day, the Strawberry and Ice Cream Festival was held and was always fun as the boys and girls roamed the cemetery behind the church while different bands played popular music and the men dipped out ice cream while the ladies sold sandwiches and cookies.

I took very seriously the things that were taught to me from the Bible and from the special services that we had with the evangelist preaching to all those present. I remember lying out in the field one night away from the lights of the buildings, and it was a very clear night with so many stars in the sky. I understood and believed that God had made all of this, and I talked to God and told him that I wanted to belong to him. On many occasions, I have thought back to that decision, and I have never regretted it. It was a personal thing, and I did not discuss it with anyone else. It is a special relationship for which I am thankful.

From that time on, I had a Friend on whom I knew I could count. I knew that He would not desert me, and many times I wondered why. I was still me and that was not always a very nice thing, yet His presence has always been there.

Sunday morning services often found three young boys in the back left corner in the smallest pew of the church. We were really snug in that seat and mischief was bound to happen. Of course, we could not make any noise and had to act like we were paying attention. What could three boys get into without making any noise! We had to do something, so we developed a game of making a fist and then seeing if another could make you open your fist by pressing down between the fingers and the knuckles. This really hurt, but we dared not yell out. We were good friends and none of us got mad as we learned how to put up with the pain.

Once a month the church ladies organization (the Women's Society) met in someone's home. The husbands would gather in the kitchen and talk and laugh about current events or talk a bit of politics. Often the kids would roam outside playing games. Most of the young girls would go to the meeting and sit more quietly than the boys could. I remember one time in the kitchen where the men were gathered and talking politics, that I heard this comment, "I wish I was a dog and Truman was a tree!" And some other jokes were also told about President Truman.

One Friday night my friend and I were playing outside the country house about ½ mile from the church, and we got into his older brother's car and found a strange looking balloon, or it seemed like a balloon. This kid, who was about two years younger than I was, took this strange balloon into the ladies' meeting. He showed it to his mother and asked her if we could play with it. That is when we make the amazing discovery that this kind of balloon was called a condom. When he came back out of the meeting, he quickly returned it to the glove compartment of his brother's car and explained to me that we had just made a big mistake! That was a learning experience for both of us. As far as we were concerned, that was the end of the story. He never did tell me what his mother actually said, but I could tell it had been something serious.

Then there was the Men's Brotherhood that was not nearly as active as the women's group. However, at one time they planted one acre of field corn to help raise money for a project at the church. They named it the Lord's Acre at the Clement's farm.

The Methodist Youth Fellowship (MYF) was for the children and was held on Sunday evenings. This was a really neat organization for young people. We would meet and have special events such as birthday parties. On one such occasion we had a party for one of the girls who was turning sixteen. As she opened her many gifts, one box finally remained. As she began to unwrap the present, it went on and on because there were many boxes inside of each other. Each one was smaller than the previous one and carefully wrapped. As the last box was unwrapped, a small nut with a note attached to it read, "To a nut, from a nut." This had been prepared by her older sister and her husband.

Meanwhile, I had been driving the farm truck and tractors all over the farm and sometimes on the rural highway that ran between Gatchellville and Muddy Creek Forks. Farm kids got to do this kind of thing, and I was very anxious to get my legal driver's license.

A year later, as Dad and I were grading some early potatoes and I was putting them on the grader from the wagon, my mother called out from the porch that a classmate and close neighbor had been killed in a tractor accident. Larry Skeleton was never to go to Kennard Dale as that school was soon to open for its first year that next month. Sadly, we would not be attending seventh grade together.

Myself in 1955.

New Life 4:

Growing Up

Our school system, where we lived, consisted of many schools. However, by 1951, schools in Pennsylvania were starting to consolidate into larger school systems with bigger and fewer high schools. In our immediate area, we Wilson kids were bused to an elementary school near Fawn Grove for first and second grades. Then we went to third through seventh grades to a school about half a mile west of Gatchellville. That building used to be the Vocational Agriculture high school in this area, but it was done away with to allow children to go to two different high schools, one in Stewartstown about 11 miles north and another in Delta about 13 miles south.

The new school district called South Eastern joined these two high schools together and would be called Kennard Dale. This newly constructed high school was located near the center of the school district and was less than one mile north of the famous Mason-Dixon Line which had separated the North and the South in previous years. The school was to house seventh grade through high school. The borders were the Susquehanna River on the east running nearly 30 miles along the Mason Dixon line to Route 83 interstate on the west. The district was about 10–15 miles wide to the North from the Mason Dixon Line. This was one of the earlier consolidations in the state that has now numbered 501 of these districts since that time. The three towns including Fawn Grove, Gatchellville, and New Park are almost a perfect triangle with about 4 1/2 miles between each of them. Only Fawn Grove has a town council, and the other two were just small villages and have remained so until today. This is still a rural area with much farm ground, but it is slowly being eaten up by houses.

    I was excited to start attending a new high school; however, the seventh grade class was only considered a junior high school. The school consisted of only one complex joined by hallways. My homeroom was #118 located on the first floor. Mrs. Blasser was to be my homeroom teacher. Each teacher had a homeroom where certain students were assigned. As the day began the roll of names was called, and each student answered "present." Being a Wilson, I fell victim to being near the end of everything that was done in any room for six years. As the teacher called out "Richard Wilson" and I replied "Present," she paused for a moment and proceeded to ask me a question. "You would not happen to be related to John Hyson Wilson would you?" I chirped back, "Yes," and asked her, "What about it?" Mrs. Blasser answered back in a firm voice, "You have two strikes against you already." As anyone could see, I was off to a roaring start for what I had been so anxious to begin. As I sat at the supper table for the evening meal, I asked my dad what he had done to Mrs. Blasser. He quickly replied that he had never heard of Mrs. Blasser. I said, "Well, she must have heard of you," and mom interrupted and told dad that she is Hazel Zellars and she married Cleo Blasser. Dad laughed and told us the story of when he was in the old Stewartstown high school and Miss Zellars was his teacher. She had told my dad that if he did not start studying harder than he now was, then he had about as much chance of passing her class as a snowball had in hell. Dad continued on to say that the next day it had started snowing, and he raised his hand and told Miss Zellars that she could get that snowball out that she was talking about yesterday. Apparently, she did not find that very amusing. My dad had not forgotten this episode even though it was over a dozen years ago, and I guess Mrs. Blasser had not forgotten it either.

    About a week into school, and again at the supper table, dad asked me this, "What is your favorite class?" I replied, "GYM class." Dad asked me, "Jim Who?" Of course, my dad had never had a gym class. We laughed, and I then answered more questions about the new school.

A Full Life or Life of a Fool

We were allowed to vote on the colors for the new school, and I never knew for sure, but I believe blue and gold won because they were the colors of the Future Farmers of America (FFA). There were a lot of us in attendance at the school at that time. Those colors remain to this day proclaiming, "Kennard Dale Blue and Gold." About that same time, the school mascot was chosen and adopted- KD Rams. We were for the most part, kids from farms, a couple of small towns, and the surrounding neighborhoods. We were all entering into a new phase of our lives where we would take on many different challenges and opportunities that we could not see coming. Mostly, this was because the school systems were rapidly changing, and our parents could not know what was coming either.

The new school was heated with coal, and the ashes were brought up in the elevator in a wheelbarrow and dumped on an old red dump truck owned by the school district. Those ashes were then screened by students and, were used to build a quarter mile track around the new football field. We were all learning how to work to improve the high school and its athletic and agricultural programs. There were other programs, but these were the two that interested me the most.

I was still making many trips to my eye doctor in York, Dr. Bruce Grove, in order to see if my crossed-eyes situation could be improved. Even though I never complained, I knew my parents wanted to fix that situation if it could be fixed. Physically I did not mind it, but mentally it did bother me a bit. I knew others were aware of the impairment, and sometimes I would hear comments about my problem. I think that because (until I was in the seventh grade) I was one of the bigger kids in the class with a fairly hot temper that it did not cause me a lot of problems. However, younger kids on the bus would make fun of me by making faces. The medical profession, or at least Dr. Grove, did not seem to know that the muscle in the weaker eye could be cut, the eye moved and straightened, and then reattached. Just by doing that could have greatly corrected the appearance problem. It seemed like I had to go there every month, and as far as I was concerned, it was a waste of time and money. I personally did not care for Dr. Grove, which did not help my situation.

At the age of sixteen, I was to get my driver's license, and in so doing I was aware that if I wore glasses, I would have to wear them forever while driving. Dr. Grove would not agree for me to do that and refused to sign a statement saying that I did not need glasses to drive. This caused me to go over the edge, and I demanded that I be permitted to go across the street to another eye doctor. My parents allowed me to do that. Mom was upset with me, but she also knew that I was upset, but she was starting to allow me to do some things on my own. Mom waited in the car while I went across the street. I had to wait a bit and then pay this doctor $15. He filled out a form for me to drive without wearing glasses. I never wore glasses to drive a car, and I know now that I did not need them to drive. My mom and dad were amazed that I had gotten that done. This incident in my life helped me to shape a personality (that most likely) was already present in my young body. Do not take no for an answer if no is not the right answer. Do not be afraid to fight for your rights or someone else's rights. Davy Crockett once said, "Make sure you are right and then go ahead!" My dad added to that phrase the following words: "And do not let any son of a bitch stop you." Dad not tell me that when I was sixteen, but sometime shortly after that. To this day, I love and respect my dad for sharing those seemingly small but important life's lessons with me.

As a teenager I was plagued with boils on different places on my body. They were very painful until they either broke open or the core was removed. One time I had ridden my two-wheeled bike up to the nearby service station for a soda pop which only cost five cents. After drinking it, I decided to mount my bike from the rear and on the run just to see how quickly I could accomplish that. For some reason, I was always trying to do something coupled with a challenge just to prove to myself that I could. At this time, I had a big and very painful boil on my butt, but I did not consider that as I tried to mount the bike without any hesitation on my part. Let me tell you, I did just that but not without some serious pain from that boil as my butt hit that seat!

I was in the local Boy Scout troop and a trip was planned to a camp in the northern part of York County about 60 miles from where we lived. As luck would have it, there had to be a medical examination to allow anyone to go to this camp. At the time I was taken to the doctor's office, I had a small but somewhat painful boil on the fourth finger of my left hand. I was not approved to go, but the boil was lanced by the doctor and quickly got better. Then I got permission to go. Even though the camp had already started, my parents made the trip late Monday just one day after the camp started. The only thing that I was restricted from doing was swimming.

Shortly after getting there, and I mean about only an hour later, I was being made fun of by the scoutmaster's son. I got into a fight with him, and I

A Full Life or Life of a Fool

tied him to a tree. When he was rescued from his plight, I was taken before a board at the camp and assigned to KP duty for the rest of the week. That meant that I would only work in the mess hall for the entire week. I liked to work, but that was not a good experience. I would never tell my parents of their wasted trip to help their wayward cross-eyed son to enjoy a week of Boy Scout camp. I might chalk that up to being born backwards. What else could it be? Because, generally, I believed that I was a normal kid.

At this time, I was about twelve. I had gotten some steel traps and started to trap for foxes, skunks, opossums, and muskrats. This was exciting because I was allowed to carry a single shot 22-caliber rifle to kill whatever I caught in my traps without being bitten before extracting the wild animal from the trap. I had several years of enjoyment catching the animals and selling them because I was making pretty good money; muskrats brought in $2.75 each. Then one morning, I noticed that where I had set three traps, I had caught a medium-sized dog. He was caught in all three traps, and I carefully got two of the traps off of his two feet. Actually, one foot was in one trap and one was on another of his legs. The last trap to get off was on his tail, of all places, and he could have just run away. However, all he would try to do was bite me when I even got close to that trap.

I knew that I would be late for school if I spent any more time on this problem, so I deducted that if I would shoot into his tail he might just simply spring out of the trap. I got the rifle close enough to his tail that I knew it would hit his tail, and sure enough, I shot and away he went. I was both happy with my accomplishment and mad at this dumb dog who was trying to bite me while I was just sincerely trying to free him. As he ran up the path that I was going to use on the way home, he then cut down across the meadow and suddenly he was coming back in my direction. I put another shell in that rifle and shot again as near to him as I could, just to let him know that I was angry with his disrespect of me while trying to rescue him from the trap. Somehow that bullet found its way to him, and I had killed the dog that I had just set free! The dog fell dead about 150 feet from me, and then I had a new problem. I did not want anyone to know about this, so I dragged this dog about 100 yards to an old junk pile that we used for tin cans and trash that would not burn. I hid him under some of those cans and quickly went off to school. Later on that year, when my uncle was hunting rabbits, I became very nervous as he got in that junk pile and started kicking around. Often times a rabbit would sit in the junk pile. But this year, there was no rabbit, and thankfully, no dog appeared.

When my dad's brother, Donald Wilson, bought a farm just a mile and a half east of our farm (I was about 12 years old), we started spending a lot of time together. The family had moved here from Arizona, and that is where their mother was from; her parents had lived there for many years. I am not sure how they got together, but they had four boys when they moved near us, and two of them were my age, and two of them were my brother's age. When we got together, we three older boys would try to get away from the three younger boys because we did not want them following us around. We did many crazy things and did not want them tattling on us. We took long hikes out across our farm land and beyond and did some things that I would rather not reveal here. Sometimes it was stupid stuff as boys are inclined to do, and we were definitely boys! We would spend a lot of time playing games like follow the leader and often times did things that were dumb and dangerous. I often wonder now if we had a death wish, or if when being that age things were done without regard to what might happen if it did not work out.

On one occasion when we were on one of our long hikes that took us past Gatchellville, I decided to challenge my two cousins to follow me while crawling through a culvert pipe that was underneath the intersection between Prospect Church Road and the road to Fawn Grove. That pipe was over 100 feet long and, at first, going into it from the bottom, the pipe was easy to crawl through. But as we got farther into the pipe, it got smaller and was not quite as easy to navigate. By the time I got about 20 feet from the upper end, I started to smell gasoline in the pipe, and there was some liquid in the bottom grooves of the pipe. My two cousins were close behind me as I was the leader of this challenge. As I continued to crawl along, all of a sudden, I saw flames from a fire that the owner of the grocery store had started in order to burn trash in the upper part of the culvert. It was just after 9:00 P.M. as he was closing the store for the evening. When I saw the fire and smelled the gasoline, I became very frightened, and I must have backed over my knees and become lodged in the pipe. I felt I was going to burn to death, and the fear of all that was to cause my body to kind of swell up, and I could not move backwards or forwards. I was completely terrified and my two cousins pulled on my ankles, but they could not free me. I was stuck for a long time, and it seemed like forever. After a certain length of time, my body must have relaxed, and I was able to free myself. We all three backed out of that culvert and never did anything like that again!

To this very day, I cannot stand to be in a tight place, and I cannot tolerate having an MRI. After a few minutes, that frightful experience comes back with a vengeance. Even an open MRI has been tried, and that does not work for me either.

Another activity we liked to do was to swing from limb to limb in the trees and play like we were Tarzan. Sometimes we would fall down to the ground. Looking back on what we had done over the years, I feel it is a wonder that we never got seriously injured. The three younger boys seemed to be satisfied to build tunnels and inside straw forts as their adventures, but they would often try to follow us. So we went far away, and then they would tend to return to the nearer farm buildings.

I remember that in the spring of the year on a very cold day, I found a mother cat and her litter of kittens in one of the forts that the other three had built. I lay there for over an hour thinking that I was helping to keep those tiny kittens warm.

At this time during my seventh and eighth grade years (which were junior high years), there were not many activities in which to participate until the senior high years which were ninth to twelfth grades. However, basketball was offered to us. Mr. Richard Prizer was the seventh and eighth grade basketball coach. He was also my favorite teacher. I believed that he knew that I loved sports, and he once told me not to take up smoking. I, being like any other student, had plenty of opportunities, but my great respect for Mr. Prizer influenced me to avoid smoking.

Mr. Prizer walked with a built-up shoe, or should I say limped with a built-up shoe because his one leg was shorter than the other. I often wondered if he befriended me because I was so cross-eyed. I never knew for sure, and I never discussed that with him, but I always felt sorry for him. One day in school he said to me that he thought he could land his plane in the big field up at the head of the lane if I thought my dad would allow him to do so. I told him that I did not think my dad would mind, and even though it was on my mind to say something to my dad that evening, I did not. Perhaps I thought it was just talk and would most likely never happen. I did know, however, that Mr. Prizer and Mr. Wetzler, a math teacher, supposedly owned an airplane that they kept at a farm about ten miles from Kennard Dale High School. At that time in history, if an airplane was near your farm and it was flying low, people would run out of their houses to see if it might be crashing.

I remember going to bed that night and thinking how neat it would be to see my favorite teacher's airplane landing in our wheat stubble field. The very next day, Mr. Prizer asked me if I would like to fly home from school. Of course, I said yes. He simply said to me that after school, instead of going home on the bus, I was to get my books and meet him at his car. We would drive down to Stewart's dairy farm where he kept the plane, and he would fly me home where he would land in the field above my house. I knew that my sister would not miss me on the bus because she was still in the elementary school in sixth grade. I, of course, was excited all day. Finally, the day ended and I got my books and jumped into that Studebaker car. We took off to the air strip. There was no way to call home and tell them what I was doing because there were no cell phones. Mr. Prizer cranked that engine up and away we went. That was my first ride in an airplane, and it was great. When we landed in the field, my dad was outside and came running out into the field. When I jumped out of that plane with my school books, anyone could have bought my dad for a nickel as he stared in amazement at what he had just seen. Mr. Prizer simply turned that plane around and took off after my thank you to him, and away he went back down to his car.

Just think of what would happen in the world now, just sixty years later, as to what might happen to a teacher who did something like that! Mr. Prizer was my favorite teacher, and I had great respect for him. We all had a pleasant talk about my good fortune at the supper table that evening.

During my eighth grade year, we students had to choose our high school path as far as academics were concerned. Of course, I chose Vocational Agriculture. I could have chosen Industrial Arts, Commercial, or College Preparatory. Some of the girls chose a course known as Home Economics.

By taking agriculture, I would have a chance to be in the FFA, the Future Farmers of America. I was so excited about this opportunity that I thought of nothing else as far as academics were concerned. I was forced by the guidance counselor Mr. William Goodling to change courses in the tenth grade as he had formulated a new course called College Preparatory Agriculture. Mr. Goodling had taken four of us agriculture students under his wing, and we all went along with the new program. It ended our study halls and gave us higher math and English courses. Mr. Goodling later became a United

States Congressman from our district in Pennsylvania. I knew it was the best thing for him to do for us. Two out of the four went to college after finishing high school. I could hardly wait for high school to start in 1954 and begin my adult life in agriculture. I did not know much, but I had big ideas.

As I entered the ninth grade, I loved every minute learning about agriculture. I was soon inducted into the FFA of Kennard Dale and was proud of our chapter which was very well-known across the state of Pennsylvania for numerous reasons. Our chapter sold farm and garden seeds in order to raise money for our chapter, and I sold enough seeds as a ninth grader to earn a trip to Florida after school was out for the summer. I could not believe that my parents allowed me to go on this trip, as I was the only ninth grader to go. We went to Daytona Beach and stayed there in a hotel resort.

What a drive that was as twenty guys took off for Florida! We did not get into any trouble, but that was probably due to more luck than good management. Our advisors, or the older folks that we were with, would drop us off at the boardwalk in the evening. Then they would go to the dog races, leaving us to ourselves to roam the beach and have a good time.

One of the requirements for agriculture was to have a home project that required keeping records. The Ag teacher was to monitor that with home visits in order to make sure that our project books were up to date. This project could vary because not all agriculture students lived on a farm. I was able to raise an acre of potatoes, an acre of corn, and maintain a swine project with several Yorkshire gilts. I had to keep a record book on each project and was graded by the Ag teacher that visited during the summer months. I loved doing this and always got near perfect grades from the Ag teacher.

Kennard Dale High School was a very upstanding place to take vocational agriculture as we had our own school farm which was all the ground on that farm that was not yet built into the high school buildings. Wilfred Bear, one of our instructors, went on to teach at the University of Delaware. This man knew swine and was instrumental in building a top herd of swine on our farm at Kennard Dale. In the mid-1950s our Yorkshire hogs won hundreds of top awards all over the state of Pennsylvania and even at the Grand National Show in Kansas City, Kansas. We had a large truck fixed up to haul the pigs and did that especially in the fall season when all the county fairs were held. Trusted students drove the truck to and from these shows and we were very successful in these endeavors.

At that time, it was acceptable at Kennard Dale for students that were involved in this activity to be allowed to miss school as long as they were busy doing this project. Each year a farm implement dealership would provide a full line of new equipment to the agriculture program for the use of farming the grounds. Ag students would assemble this machinery in the winter months and then farm the school fields with it the next year. Then some other dealer would bring a different brand of equipment for the next year.

One year we bought a cage layer chicken house at the PA Farm Show, and the Ag students tore it down, hauled it from Harrisburg to our farm at Kennard Dale, and rebuilt it to be used to house laying chickens and sell the eggs. This was a lot of work, and the Ag teachers worked hard with the students to accomplish this feat. Some of the fathers of Ag students got involved and were also a big help. These were volunteers who just loved their children and loved the Kennard Dale FFA chapter.

One day as my class went down to the farm to work during class time, we had a substitute teacher by the name of George Grove. He was quite a character himself, and he also had a cage layer house for chickens. He was good friends with our regular Ag teachers. This day we were going to grade potatoes, and as we gathered at the cellar under the barn, someone had found a used condom. We filled it with water and hung in on a nail which was used to hang the extension cord for the light. This was over the potato grader. It must have had at least a half-gallon of water in it. It was bobbing up and down as Mr. Grove came into the cellar, and he yelled who the hell did that. Just as he yelled, that condom busted and water flew all over him and much laughter was heard. No one got in trouble even though we all got chewed out. Anyone who saw that would never forget it.

After I got my driver's license in 1957, I drove my 1949 Chevy to school every day in order to get home quickly and get to work on the farm. While at school we were allowed to drive our cars, at least those who had cars, down to the farm for Ag class. Believe me when I say that Ag students really ruled the roost at that time at KD, but that was soon to change. More kids prepared for college, and the push from the government was for that to continue. I was usually the first kid to leave school when we were dismissed for the day. I sped out as quietly and quickly as I could in order to get home as soon as I could. I never stopped for the stop sign that was near the back of the auditorium because all the buses were lined up in the front of the school, and there was no traffic there until the buses pulled out.

A Full Life or Life of a Fool

One day several of my classmates tied a piece of 1 ¼ inch galvanized pipe that was 21 feet long to the back of my Chevy. I knew it was there and warned them that they better get it off. When the bell rang, I was out of there. I took off with this piece of pipe dragging behind as they had tied it on with binder twine. As I rounded the auditorium, lo and behold, the principal Mr. Webb was standing there watching me. When I saw him, I hit my brakes and the section of pipe passed me like I was sitting still. The twine tore into two parts, and the pipe went flying through the air. Even though I knew it had missed him by a few feet, I simply stopped at the stop sign and went on home, as if all was well. It was not until the next morning when school opened and the announcements were made over the intercom that word came out that all Ag students with cars could not drive their cars anywhere on school property until school was over for the day.

One morning before school started as the janitor was bringing up the ashes from the basement in order to dump them on the school truck, I noticed something was wrong with the large steel door that raised up on top of the rounded steel beam on top of the elevator to a nearly straight up position by the window in our Ag homeroom. This lid would then slide back down into a closed position as the elevator continued down into the basement. I could tell that the lid at the up position could be easily held as it was nearly centered and easy to hold. So I got the bright idea to hold the door by hand and not let it go down. The janitor in the elevator would be confused and come back up, at which time I would either release the lid, or I could hold it and really confuse him as to what was going on with it. No harm, no foul as far as I could tell. That lid weighed well over several hundred pounds, but it was easy to hold. So I held it, and as the elevator went down the janitor stopped it as I figured he would. At that time another student suddenly yelled, "Webb is coming." He was the principal and that foiled my plans. I suddenly pushed the lid and down it went. When it hit the top of that rounded part of the elevator, there was a loud crashing noise of steel on steel, and the noise echoed throughout the school. Several minutes later, the janitor came out of the basement stairs yelling that he was burned by a hot light bulb that had broken when the lid came crashing down on the steel beam. The broken glass had gone down inside his shirt. This prank had really backfired. I was pissed at the guy that caused me to drop the lid because Mr. Webb had not really been coming. I quickly admitted to what had happened, and took the blame. I received a good licking from the principal's paddle, with which I was already familiar. I then, on my own, asked for forgiveness from the janitor. He was not a very happy camper and seemed to think it was not very funny; however, later on we became good friends in life.

I got my share of lickings during my school years, and I can honestly say that I deserved all of them. I left school with no bad feelings for any teacher except the one biology teacher who claimed his brother-in-law down in New Jersey had chickens that laid two or three eggs per day. I knew he was lying and told my dad that he should be banned from teaching. I loved agriculture and math but did not have much desire to excel in any other subject. However, all this was to soon change as the US education system was insisting on more academics and less agriculture.

Little did I realize at that time, that I would be elected to that same school's district board of directors some forty years later. At that time, I would have to sit in judgment of children that had done wrong things, and I would have to approve of the discipline that they were being given by their administrators.

New Life 5:

Getting Ready to Step Out Into the World

In my junior year at Kennard Dale in 1957, I would be spending a whole week away from school along with several other students at the York Interstate Fair. We slept in the top of the hog barn over top the pigs. We slept on board bunks supplied with straw and sleeping bags. During the day, we fed the animals and worked on preparing our pigs for the different classes. We had a really neat project exhibit, and we won first place in the Big Exhibit contest.

We had about 15 small piglets, perhaps two weeks old, that were being fed by a machine that had nipples attached. We had to keep the special formula very fresh, and the nipples had to be cleaned several times a day. Not keeping them clean would cause the piglets to get scours and die. This was a hard exhibit to take care of, but the people loved it; and it was truly the eye-catcher of the fair that year.

Lots of unusual things happened at the fair as many people flowed through the livestock buildings. We were very busy, but we also had much fun as we worked with our pigs. I had my own Yorkshire gilt at the fair, and I worked with her as well as with the big herd of Yorkshire pigs that belonged to the Kennard Dale FFA chapter.

The previous year when I was a sophomore, I had a Berkshire gilt at the fair as well. I won her by writing an essay sponsored by Sears & Roebuck. The name of the contest was "Why I Want to Own a Sears & Roebuck Gilt." Because I won, I was awarded the gilt that came from the last year's essay winner. I, in turn, had to give one to the next year's winner, and I did. However, I had very bad luck with the gilt that I won. I had to spend more on vet bills than I could possibly make back. So I sold her after her first litter and gave away the one gilt that survived.

Just for the record, a gilt is a female pig that has not had a litter of baby pigs. When the first litter is born, she then becomes a sow. Of course, the male is a boar, and if he is castrated, he becomes a barrow and will be fattened for slaughter. Yorkshire is a breed and so is Berkshire, Hampshire, Landrace, Duroc, and Spotted Poland China, to name a few of the more popular breeds.

I began to wash my Yorkshire gilt and got her ready to show. Being a white breed, she had white hair. By putting Johnson's baby powder on her it brought out her appearance even more and made her look good. Part of getting her ready to show is to make sure she catches the judge's eye. My gilt went on to win first place, but something much more important was in the air.

Some high school girls from another school by the name of Dallastown were visiting the fair that Monday. Schools had off that day to visit the York Fair since the fair catered to education- particularly homemaking, sewing, animal raising, crop raising and other contests in which the students could participate. Money was paid out for prizes, and there were many students competing for the prizes. The local newspaper would publish the names of all the winners and the amounts won.

This one girl kind of caught my eye as she was passing through the fair. She had a scarf on her head, and I grabbed it and took off thinking she would chase me. She only scowled at me, and I felt forced to return and apologize to her. Little did I know that this girl would someday be my wife, and in fewer than three years. More than that, we neither one had remembered that we had first met in the York Hospital in July of 1940, seventeen years before in the baby ward. Remember our mothers, who did not know one another, were there at the same time, and so were we! I only knew that there was a special attraction that I had for this girl of ninety pounds. Soon the girls left; but they returned one evening later in the week and we got to talk for a bit. They agreed that they would return again on Friday evening.

My first official date with this girl with a strange first name was on Saturday of that week. DeEtta Elaine Godfrey was her name, and she lived at 23 South Park Street in Dallastown. I had thought very carefully about asking her for that first date, and I knew it would be a different situation because of my father owning a truck. I was supposed to take home five gilts, including my own, in that truck and deliver them to their respective farms. So I carefully asked her if she would like to go along with me in the truck as I delivered the gilts, and she said yes. On Saturday evening I drove my '49 Chevy thirty miles to my home farm and switched to the blue Chevy that we mostly used to haul potatoes. Now I would have my first date including delivering five different gilts to other Kennard Dale FFA students from our chapter. I picked up my date at her house around 7:00 P.M. and assured her mom and dad that she would be home no later than 11:00 p.m.

DeEtta Godfrey, the love of my life; her senior picture.

Things went well, and we talked as I drove onto the fair grounds. I loaded the gilts and headed south on the trip to the farm to unload each gilt. All was well until one of the gilts got off at the wrong farm and headed away from the buildings. I gave chase, and some two hours later returned to the truck with the gilt. At the next stop, I had the same problem. By the time I left that stop with my date just sitting in the truck, it was already time for her to be home. I still had my gilt on the truck and had five miles to go to my house where my car was parked. I decided to leave my gilt on the truck until morning and get this girl up the road. It was already past midnight, and we were still twenty minutes from Dee's home (Dee is what I learned to call her.) We both jumped into my car, and as I drove up the road my mind was racing. I really liked this girl, and I just knew that I would never get to know her any better because I would most likely never see her again. Doing some fast thinking while I was at the stop sign at Stamper Road and Route 74, I decided to get her to take my school ring. That way I would at least get to see her one more time in order to get the ring back. So as we were stopped, I asked her if she would indeed like to have my school ring. She said that she would like that, so I gave it to her and continued up the road.

Arriving in Dallastown at her house, I felt somewhat relieved as at least I got her safely home. She thanked me for the evening, and I went down the road thinking that I had made a wise decision about my class ring. She has had that ring for sixty-two years and has never given it back yet! At this time neither one of us knew that we had been born at the same hospital so near the same time. Fate is an amazing thing, and here we were back together many years later. Eventually, we would be married at the tender age of nineteen in 1959.

Also while at the York Fair that year, a drunk came by and took one of the small pigs. The owner from Western Pennsylvania was not there at the time, but some of us FFA boys made sure that the man left empty-handed and a bit bruised up.

We had a big Yorkshire boar hog, and he weighed over 900 pounds. There was also a Burlesque show up on the Midway which was about a 100 yard walk from the hog barn. We plotted to send a couple of guys into the show. They got Donnie the big boar hog out of his pen. By using several hurdles (those were pieces of ply wood with handles cut in them) Donnie could be made to go wherever he was steered. Several of us walked Donnie around the exhibitors' trucks so that we did not cause a lot of attention. We eased him near the Burlesque show tent, and at the appointed time, the two guys inside the tent, lifted the flap and we ran Donnie in and got him worked up by speeding up his walk. We all yelled, "Wild boar!" Donnie made a couple of really loud "BOFS, BOFS," and the people quickly emptied the tent. The nearly naked performer screamed along with others and that show was over! We quickly

A Full Life or Life of a Fool

ushered Donnie out of the tent and back to his pen at the hog barns. We really had no trouble doing that; however, most all of the people in that tent, except for us, had no idea that this was a planned event by some really mischievous FFA students from Kennard Dale High School. It was not long after, that the police came into the hog barn to investigate the situation. Of course, all of us were anxious that Donnie had gotten out, but we rescued him from the Burlesque tent and got him safely back into his pen. I know the policemen thought it was a big story, but how could they arrest a bunch of boys just doing their civic duty! We were very straight forward with them. I think they were shaking their heads as they left and most likely had a lot of conversations about that afterwards.

Besides learning how to get late night snacks for nothing out of the Rutter's ice cream freezer after the fair closed for the night, we also learned how to use a piece of binder twine off of the straw bales to cut them and tie them together to make a longer rope. We then would tie it around the trip lever in the dunking machine so we could be a long way in back of the exhibit while it was operating, and we could dunk the guy on the seat anytime we wanted. We would have one of our guys throw balls and just pull the string when the ball hit the back stop. Even if it missed, the guy got dunked, and we got many free teddy bears before they caught on to what we were doing!

Very late one evening, but before the fair closed for the night, I was awakened from my straw bunk. I was in my sleeping bag with only my underpants on, and one of the older students told me to get up and just put my coveralls on. We were all going to get a picture taken in a jailhouse stand that was selling pictures. They had a bunch of big whiskey bottles to really make it look like the real thing. Being young and dumb I just pulled on my coveralls and away I went. Now up in the Midway, about eight of us got in this makeshift jailhouse to have this picture taken. They pulled my coveralls down for the picture, so I had no shirt on and just held my coveralls at the waist for the picture. One of these guys was Charlie Winemiller, who by the way, was the president of our FFA chapter. Charlie became a dear friend of mine and worked both for me and with me many years later. Two of these guys were from another neighboring high school which was Lower Chanceford. Later, after consolidation, it became part of the Red Lion School District. That was the last year for Lower Chanceford to have an FFA chapter.

Picture at the 1956 York Fair, KD FFA and Lower Chanceford FFA boys.

Many years later as I served as president of the South Eastern School District, I was visiting the elementary school in Delta. I was reading a book to some children in a special class when the fifth grade teacher asked me if I could identify some people in a picture that she had. She was the daughter of one of the FFA guys in that picture from long ago. She recognized me, but her dad could not identify two of the other students because they were from Chanceford. I identified both of them, and she was so anxious to tell her dad. He had kept that picture all these years, and the family was just looking at it the night before. Miss Grove had brought it to school that day. Amazingly, I still had my picture and continue to have it to this day! We had a lot of good memories from the York Fair. These had been exciting times, but the most important thing that happened was meeting my wife-to-be for the second time in my life.

The last couple of years of high school were busy years as our family farming operation now included growing strawberries along with the potatoes. Mom and Dad had started selling produce that we were raising on our farm.

In the yard on the picnic table, mom would have a display. Many neighbors and friends came to buy the nice vegetables that we had for sale. Mom was extremely busy with outside work as our youngest sister was now seven years old and able to be out and about the farm.

I remember one night after the graduation service at Kennard Dale for one of my cousins, that it was supposed to get very cold that night, and frost was predicted for the morning. The frost would ruin the strawberry blossoms, so most of the family worked all night hauling some old wheat straw out of the bottom of the straw moll in the barn. This turned out to be a disaster because of all the old wheat seeds in that straw. All of a sudden, we had a wheat field instead of a strawberry patch. A big lesson was learned! After that, Dad would just leave enough of the wheat straw in the field, and he would rake it up into big windrows and let the wheat that was left in the straw to sprout out. By the middle of November or December, we would then load the straw on the wagon and spread it on the strawberry field. This worked so well that we continued it for many years. Good wheat straw mulch for the winter and moving it between the rows in the early spring, made a nice cushion for the knees while picking the berries. This also caused the berries to be cleaner and even put a glisten on the appearance of them as they were put into the boxes. A few years later, we bought an irrigation system and were able to prevent the strawberry blossoms from being frosted and ruined during the months of April through mid-May.

My father John Wilson, much like his father Charles, had a green thumb. This meant that he was able to raise beautiful vegetables on our farm during a time when this was becoming more and more important to our livelihood. From the time that I planted a lima bean in my nose, and later planted peanuts in the garden as a Boy Scout project, I loved to see things grow. I loved experimenting to see what would cause the food to be better and yield a bigger crop.

At age fifteen in 1955, I planted six stalks of potatoes in a choice part of our garden, which Dad permitted me to do. I planted them exactly the same day as we planted the whole field just next to the garden. As they came out of the ground, they looked the same as the ones in the field and soon they began to blossom. This is the time when they start the little tubers under the ground which later grow into potatoes of all sizes. Even though both the field and the garden were beautiful at this time, I started carrying water to my six stalks. Using a syringe, I would inject perhaps a cup of water into the ground around each plant every day I injected the water because I did not want the ground to get hard or crusted on the top as it was getting hot by this time. The sun would bake the top of the ground if it was wet. It did not rain much in the month of June, and the field alongside of the garden looked really dry. My project of six plants had grown larger than those in the field and also looked fresher and healthier. I had to scratch down in the soil around one of the plants, and I very carefully did not disturb the tubers that had already started to grow into potatoes-some more than an inch and a half around. As the next week or so went on, I also sneaked out in the field so as not to be seen by my dad because he always told me not to mess around with the potatoes while they were growing. I dug around a couple of places in that field and could not find any potatoes at all. At that time, I had never seen my dad pull up a hill of potatoes in a field until near time to harvest them.

On the other hand, for several years, I would sneak out at the backside of the farm where I could not be seen, and I would pull up a potato stalk just to look at its roots and try to figure out how all this worked. I was fascinated with the details of this crop. Then I would replant the stalk in the ground thinking I would not get caught. I did not know that you could not replant a potato stalk. I was very nervous one evening at the supper table when Dad brought up the fact that some of the potatoes in the field at the other end of the farm were dying. He was afraid that they may have had a disease and would all die. So I learned at that time that I would have to change the way I handled the pulling up of a potato stalk. From that time on, I would pull up the stalk, spread the stalks that were next to that one, and then carry that stalk to the cornfield where I could discard it without leaving any evidence. I really felt I had to do this thing of checking because I was so interested. Even though I was warned not to, the threat of the family not making it financially because of not being able to pay the bills was so great that I could not stand it. And besides, I wanted to do that, and being the wayward kid that I was, I figured out how to do it without getting caught.

My dad took things seriously and was, I am sure, under a lot of pressure. In agriculture a farmer can do a good job, or the weather can turn sour, or a disease can wipe out the crop. Then all that money is invested and there is nothing to pay the bills. Sometimes gloom and doom would be the topic of the evening meal. I always hated that and would try to say something encouraging to change the subject or inject some humor into the meal time conversation.

A Full Life or Life of a Fool

As June came to an end and no rain was falling from the sky, I had to make a move that I knew would be hard to accomplish. Even though my dad did not say anything about the difference between my six stalks in the garden and those in his field, I just knew he had to be noticing and thinking about it. I do not know if he had done any scratching around my six stalks or not because at that time he was so very much against digging up or pulling up a stalk of potatoes.

Finally, at the evening meal one evening when the dry weather was being discussed, I sprang the deal to my dad. I said, "Dad, after supper I want you to go out in your field next to the garden and pull out the best stalk of potatoes that you think will have on it the most potatoes. Then we will go to my six stalks and you can pull out whichever one you want, and we will compare what we find." Dad would not agree to this, but the next morning he came to me and said, "Let's go out in the field and pull up a stalk." I knew he would pull up a stalk that had only one vine because he knew it would have a bigger potato on it because that is the way it usually worked. Now, remember, when the seed piece is planted in the ground, if it only has one good eye, there will only be one vine out of that seed piece. If it has no eyes, that seed piece will remain in the ground, and it will stay there until it rots and no vine. If it has more eyes, there may be two or three or sometimes four vines. A one vine stalk is called a single stalk, and, sure enough, that is what my dad chose. As he pulled it and scratched the ground to see what he could find in the hole that it came out of, there were only three potatoes still clinging to the vine. He scratched and scratched, but no potatoes could be found. Worst of all, the three that were still clinging to the vine, were smaller than ping pong balls. I will never forget his comment. "Not much here!"

We walked some 150 feet to get out of the field and into my garden. Dad said, "Okay, you pull one up." I told Dad, "You pick it." He did, and I gently pulled the stalk that had three vines and many potatoes on it. I then dug up five potatoes that were already US #one in size. That means they were nearer the size of a baseball, and there were seven more about the size of ping pong balls. Some smaller potatoes were still growing. I had not planted any single stalks because I did not want big potatoes; I wanted lots of potatoes.

My dad had tears in his eyes and was totally amazed. He was so impressed that after talking with Mom, he made a call to Hyde Dooley the local dealer for irrigation systems and ordered one. They would send an engineer out to spec the system in a few days. Then he called the bank realizing that he would have to borrow some money if he was going to do this. He immediately got in touch with a gentleman that lived in Gatchellville by the name of George Brooks. This man was a pond builder and owned heavy equipment. Within several days, we had two ponds built. The engineer had come from Olin Matheson Company, a guy by the name of Dick Curran. He was really more of a salesman with a device to run on the top of the ground to see how much pipe we needed to buy. He was from a small village about 10 miles away known as Collinsville. He had grown up on the family farm there. He went to college and now had a good job selling fertilizer and irrigation equipment. I really liked this guy, and he and I spent a lot of time together doing this project.

He designed the system with a Chrysler Industrial straight six-cylinder gasoline engine. It was to pump many millions of gallons of water for my dad and performed nearly perfectly. It was later sold along with the rest of the equipment as Dad got into his early eighties and decided to quit raising vegetables.

Mr. Curran told me we would use four-inch aluminum pipe for the sprinklers and five-inch pipe for the main line. He showed me how he calculated the friction loss and determined the elevation from the water supplies. All these figures caused us to use the proper size pipe. Then Mr. Dick, as I called him, told me we just had one more thing to do which was to measure the distance from the water supply to the farthest spot on the farm which would be the main line. The sprinkler line was to be determined by the length of the longest setting for the longest field. That was what this wheel which he ran along the ground would determine. When we got ready to measure, I told him that I had already stepped it off, and I knew that we would need 46 pieces of four-inch line and 55 pieces of five-inch line. He chuckled a little bit and said that meant we needed 23 sprinklers. He calmly said that if he did not do his job right, he might get fired; so he was going to measure it anyway. I wanted to get this done so we could start pumping water. I had already stepped the distance, but I followed along as Mr. Dick did his job. When he got done, he told me that I was almost right. So I asked him, "Where am I off?" He explained that we needed 47 pieces of four-inch line because there had to be an extra pipe on the end of the line to catch any debris that might be in the pipe. If not, it might clog up the last sprinkler. I understood that, and Mr. Dick and I became close friends. When I started farming, I bought an irrigation system from his company and much fertilizer. I know he was shocked that my measurements had been so close to being exact because I heard him tell my dad.

A Full Life or Life of a Fool

Dad knew I was very interested in what was going on and was trusting me more to make some decisions.

Dad had called the bank, and they sent three directors of the bank to the farm to discuss Dad borrowing the money. I knew that I did not need to be in that discussion, but I was listening intently as they quizzed my dad. I had my fingers crossed because I knew we needed to get water on our crops and quickly. I remember one of the men said to my dad, "John, you are asking for more money than what you paid for this farm." My dad replied, "I know it is too much money, but that is the price of the equipment, and I need water on these crops." They talked among themselves for a few minutes, and I heard them say they were going to loan Dad the money. I wanted to yell out, but knew I dare not. It was a happy supper that evening, and the equipment started arriving in a day or two. Then we went to work putting water on the crops.

The crops responded quickly, and we were able to salvage a much better yield than we would have had without the system. That system was used every year for some of the crops. As Dad had a green thumb and really understood plants, he was quickly raising vegetables that needed some extra water at times during the summer dry spells. Before Dad quit farming, and as he sold that irrigation system to a farmer from up above Harrisburg, he told me that that piece of equipment made him more money than anything else he had ever bought. It was still worth about what he paid for it some 35 years before.

Down at Muddy Creek Forks there is a popular trout stream. The Keiser family had come there in the 1940s, and they had children about our age. We occasionally went down there on a Saturday evening for groceries, and Dad bought some coal and fertilizer from Mr. Keiser. I loved to get with the two sons and hunt bullfrogs in the mill race that used to power the old mill. These bullfrogs were huge and made a lot of noise.

Also, in Muddy Creek Forks lived the brother of my eye doctor, and his name was Freddie Grove. He had some physical problems and never worked but was kept by the Jones family, who lived in a house down back of the mill. It seemed he was always in the store because he lived close by, and most likely, had nothing else to do. He was kind of a fixture because he was always there. He was happy and cheerful and never caused any trouble. The Grove family paid the Jones family to keep Freddie, and he lived with them for many years.

The Ma and Pa Railroad ran through Muddy Creek Forks, and there was a post office in the store that the Keiser family ran. Mrs. Keiser worked as the postmaster, tended the store, and helped run the mill. The Keiser family lived over top the store which was accessed by a big wooden set of stairs that ran up at the back of the store. It was a very large building and is still standing. It is part of the historic Ma and Pa Railroad Society.

The reason the area was called Muddy Creek Forks is because two large streams came together there by the store and mill. One stream that came from the North near Red Lion, and the other came from the West near Stewartstown. This water flows into the Susquehanna River just above Delta.

Over the years, there have been major floods there. The water often flowed through the bottom part of the house and up near the porch. On the wall there are high water marks from certain years.

Down the stream from there was a crossing on the creek known as Bruce. My Uncle Donald Wilson's farm was just up over the hill from there. Sometimes my two cousins Don and Roger and myself would hike the railroad tracks and just mess around. Once we found a large hornet nest on a pole next to the tracks, and we heaved stones at the nest. We would then run away so as not to get stung. We quickly found out that the hornets were smart and could follow the flight of the stone. We were not near as smart as we thought we were. A hornet packs a wallop as it stings, and that experiment did not work too well.

I took my driver's test on my sixteenth birthday since I got my learner's permit thirty days before which was the law. I passed the first time as I had been driving the truck for a long time. I do not think the policeman appreciated the fact that I was just sixteen that day, but he did not fail me. This was also the end of my seeing Dr. Grove, and I did not wear glasses again until later in life. Then at age 50, I started wearing contact lenses and have worn them to this day.

In my seventeenth year of life after reuniting with my babyhood sweetheart (now my wife of 60 years), I took my now girlfriend to visit my Wilson grandparents. I knew that Grandpa and Grandma had gotten a television set, not because they wanted one, but because Grandma's brother from Phoenix, Arizona, had visited her recently. My grandparents were in their late 70s and would never have purchased a TV as both of them thought they were evil, sinful, undesirable inventions of this now messed up world.

Before leaving to go back to Phoenix, my Uncle Walter Bartol and Grandma's brother went to a TV dealer and paid him cash to put in a new TV and an antenna on the house. But they were not to install it until they left town.

The guy must have done a good job of selling himself to Grandma because he got it delivered and installed and none of the family could figure out how.

Grandma despised her brother Walter because he had married an American Indian in Arizona. We never heard her say anything good about her brother, who was now a wealthy rancher and land owner in the West. Now Dee and I were going to visit Grandpa and Grandma unannounced so I could check out how the TV thing was going. I turned my car lights off as we entered the driveway so we could get on the porch without their knowledge. Sure enough, they were sitting in there together watching that "evil appliance." We were so amused and watched them for a while, but because it was cold outside we finally knocked on the door. Grandma jumped up and turned off the TV and quickly came to the door. We went in and said our hellos, and before I sat down I asked how they liked their new TV. Grandpa did not say anything, but Grandma blurted out that it was an awful thing and should not be in their house. As I walked past and rubbed the TV, I simply stated, "Wow, it is nice and warm!" In our couple of hours visit, not one other word was mentioned about the TV. As the years went by, Grandpa loved to watch professional wrestling on the screen. He would have never believed that any of it was fake. He was just excited to watch, and Grandma did not want to ever hear his conversations about it.

My junior and senior years were flying by, and I was busy at school, home, and now had a new interest in Dee that quickly became my chief interest.

I had been entered into the Star Farmer contest from the Kennard Dale FFA chapter. I had also just been selected, after much competition from other chapters in several other counties, as the Star Farmer from that area. I was awarded an all-expenses paid trip to Kansas City, Missouri, in the spring of the year. Several Ag students from other schools also went along with Mr. Leamer and me in his big Buick. We had a great time, and we all very proudly wore our Blue and Gold FFA jackets with our names and our awards that we had won over the past few years.

While in Kansas, a bunch of guys from some of the other areas and states decided to walk across the bridge to Kansas City, Kansas, in order to visit the stockyards and whatever else we could find on the other side of the Mississippi River. What we found was a gang of bad ass teenagers who did not appreciate us new people in town.

Shortly, just before an encounter with these guys, several police cars showed up, and we were ushered back across the river to our hotel. The officers told us that these guys did not like our blue coats and we were not to come back into that neighborhood again.

Later on in the week, we were taken to the stockyards and given a tour that was supervised without incident. I was amazed at how many steers were being slaughtered in a short period of time. They killed the steer by chaining their heads into position, and three black men were using sledge hammers to kill them. It seemed a bit crude to me as I thought they would shoot them, but this assembly line seemed to be quite efficient, and so it was.

On the way home, we stopped at the big Purina Research farm near St. Louis, Missouri, and we observed how the color of the yoke of an egg could be changed. This was simply done by adding cake coloring to their feed. They broke open eggs on a white plate and one would be red, the next one blue, and then green. The shell was still white. I learned a lot on that trip. Later on, we stopped at a restaurant, and Mr. Leamer asked one of the guys to get him an ashtray off of a lady's table as she sat there smoking, alone. She yelled at him, and he quickly replaced the ashtray and walked out of the restaurant feeling very embarrassed. He did not return.

Between my junior and senior years before we left for summer break, one of the FFA students and an officer by the name of Kermit Miller, gave me a set of Gordon Horseshoes. He told me to practice up over the summer so I could take his place in a particular event. This event was a track meet held by the County FFA each year with many different contests, such as volleyball, land judging, cattle judging and several other events. If a person won at the county level, then he could go to the area level which included perhaps five counties. If he won there, he would get to go to Penn State University to the Pa. Annual Ag Days Celebration and then compete for the state championship.

I was fortunate enough to win the local competition and advanced to the state, and then won the FFA state championship in 1958. It was much fun. On the way home, the Ag teacher that was with us took us to his father-in-law's farm, and we helped put away hay for his dairy cows before leaving for York County and home.

My senior year found me thinking of many things-my girlfriend of whom I was very fond, my dad and the farm that would be waiting for me after graduation, and the threat of being drafted by the military because of my age. I wanted to farm in the worst way, but the threat of military service could mess me up just as I would start to farm. I decided to consult with a

A Full Life or Life of a Fool

Marine Corp recruiting officer at my high school. I talked it over with Dee and decided to join. Most Marine enlistments were for four years, but they were offering a three-year enlistment, and I could leave whenever I wanted to within nine months after graduation. I signed up while still in high school to leave as soon after Christmas as they wanted me to go. They took me on December 28 of 1958.

My dad was really upset because he had just bought a new International 350 Utility Tractor with a three bottom plow. He later told me he thought that if he bought it, I would stay on the farm. But he had failed to tell me that, and it would not have made any difference. I was a head strong young guy who was anxious to do what I wanted to do, and I had already made up my mind. However, I had talked it over with the love of my life, and we were both thinking of the future and getting this military obligation out of the way.

Near graduation, I got a call from a neighbor farmer who was a big time potato farmer and the most progressive farmer in our area. It just so happened that he was the father of the girl that I kissed while in first grade and got into a peck of trouble in school. I do not know if he ever knew about that incident. I had never been in the McPherson's house which was less than ½ mile from our farm. Mr. Hugh McPherson owned most of the land that nearly surrounded our farm and the McCleary farm across from us. So I am sitting in his living room and he is about to surprise me. Mr. McPherson had a stuttering problem and when he got excited it was worse, and he was an excitable man. As he started to talk to me, he said the following, "Boy, I got big plans for you. I am going to give you a job here and some day you will be running this whole operation." I was flattered by the offer, but calmly explained to him that I had already joined the Marine Corps. He immediately stuttered out, "WHAT THE HELL, HELL, HELL, DID YOU DO THAT FOR?" That was pretty much the end of my first job and that conversation. I never spoke to him again as he died a fairly young man from a heart attack. His children and grandchildren continue to own and operate that farm and many others.

Before I graduated from Kennard Dale, I was on the honor roll because of my good grades. I was a trusted student, and as Mr. Schuman was my Ag teacher and my homeroom teacher, he had me do the attendance roll every day. I would mark myself present in the official book, and if I wanted to go home and work I would include my name on the absentee list that went to the office. When it was printed out with my name on it, no teacher expected me in that class that day. I would simply leave school in my car and drive home and go to work. Sometimes my dad would ask me why I was home, and I would just say that I was working on my projects, and that was good enough for Dad as he loved having me home working. Not much was ever said, and I had done this perhaps 20 times and gotten away with it.

One day that I could have been home legally because I was getting chickens ready for a Chicken of Tomorrow Contest, I got found out. I was putting the chicks out of the box of 50 that had just arrived in the little brooder house across from our house. We always dipped each of their beaks into the water fountain thinking that would teach them where the water was. I had just finished the last chick, and suddenly there came a loud knock on the door. As I unhooked the door and looked out, there stood Mr. Howel, the principal. I immediately went on the offensive and scolded him for scaring my little peeps with his loud knock. I told him I would be out when I finished what I was doing. I watched him through a knothole in one of the siding boards, and he was walking up and down the lane in front of the brooder house and rubbing his hands together. I knew he did that when he was mad. After five minutes or so, I decided to go out and face the music.

Mr. Howel apologized to me for scaring my chicks and told me the following: "I don't care if you are on the honor roll or not, but if you miss one day the rest of this year, you will not walk in your graduation, and you better not get sick or you will not walk!" I thanked him and took his words of wisdom very seriously and did not miss another day. I do not think my dad ever found out, and I continued to take the roll for Mr. Schuman. Nothing was ever said to me again, and I did not ask any questions.

Before that incident and earlier in the year, a bunch of us kids had hooked school, and they all went to the movies, but I went home to work. The punishment was all the same. I got no break for going home to work.

Graduation did not seem to mean a whole lot to me, and I do not remember who spoke. I had loved parts of school, but my English teacher knew me well. She wrote in my yearbook as she signed her picture, "To a student very often missing from the first seat in the third row, Florence Seaks." I was listed in the yearbook class prophecy as being given a speeding ticket on Route 74 by another student George Corbett who was the make believe state policeman. Thus ended my high school years.

New Life 5A:

Off to the Military

I said my good-byes to all my family at Christmas and to my sweetheart, Dee. I boarded a train in York, PA, bound for Philadelphia where I would be sworn in to the Marines at the post office building. Because my last name was Wilson, I was nearly the last one to go forward to sign the paperwork. When they called my name, I went forward and looked down on the paperwork that I was to sign and was told, "Boy, those papers are to sign, not to read." I just hurriedly kept on reading, and I could see that there were many places that said there were four years to serve and not three as I expected. As the Marine yelled at me again to sign, I simply headed out the door, walked down the street, and would have gone home except two Marines approached me and said there had been a mistake. They told me to just come back up and they would fix the papers. I returned inside with them, and it took about 45 minutes, but I was given a whole bunch of pages to sign with a whole bunch of three years written on them, and then I signed.

My cousin who had already signed his papers and was supposed to have the same three-year program as I did, wound up serving four years because he signed the wrong papers. He had already been in college for two years and had ROTC. I was cross-eyed, but I could see even though I was only looking out of one eye which I did not realize at the time. I am sure that I would have found my way back home if they would not have changed the paperwork. I was young and green, but I would stand my ground when necessary.

As I rode another train to South Carolina to Parris Island, I was wondering what I might do if things did not work out right. As we got somewhere near to Parris Island during the midnight hours, they put us in what I would call a shed that had some bunks, but no mattress pads, just springs. I climbed up on one of them and fell asleep. Not for long though, because I heard yelling and cussing and Billy clubs banging on the steel of the bunks. They were herding us out of that building to get on a bus to go the last leg of the journey to Parris Island. I simply tried to stay in the middle of the pack so the billy clubs would not strike me. I remember as I went out the door that I stepped on the side of somebody's face who had apparently fallen. It was really dark, but I just kept going, got on the bus, and shortly we arrived at Parris Island.

We got rid of our clothing and packed it up to be sent home. We were issued new uniforms that consisted of utilities, and a hat that had to be called a cover and new underwear. We were led to the barracks and got dressed in our new clothing. Next, we were ushered outside to be with many other recruits who had come in from all over the country. By this time our heads had been totally shaved, and we all pretty much looked the same. There must have been about 300 of us in that group. A Marine in dress blues and with a swagger stick came walking up, jumped on a stump so all of us could see him, and shouted out these exact words which I shall never forget. "YOU MAGGOTS ARE LOWER THAN WHALE SHIT, AND WHALE SHIT IS FOUND AT THE BOTTOM OF THE OCEAN. YOUR HEART AND SOUL MAY BELONG TO GOD, BUT FOR THE NEXT SIXTEEN WEEKS YOUR ASS BELONGS TO ME!" Those words were 100% true, and I never regretted joining and having the experiences that I had for the next three years. I have always respected the military since that time.

Because of being so cross-eyed, the drill instructors picked that up right away. I was given the name of "interlocking bands of grazing eyesight" and was told that I would never qualify with an M1 Rifle. The guys that were our platoon drill instructors wanted to get meritorious promotions with the graduating of each platoon. To have someone not qualify with the M1 Rifle was not a good thing for them. So they dwelt on me with my bad eyes, thinking how to get rid of me so I would not pull the platoon down. The harder they

A Full Life or Life of a Fool

picked on me, the harder I fought back. The only advantage I had was that they could not tell which eye I was looking out of, and that really distressed them. This gave me the only out I had, and I used it to help keep me feeling that I was in control. Sometimes one of them would walk up next to me while I was at attention and say, "Wilson, if I thought you were eyeballing me, I would knock you down." I would say nothing even though I was looking right at him with one eye. One of the things that we did every day was to run five miles with our M1's. The instructor who would lead us was always Sergeant Chase. He told us to run up his ass and stay close. I ran the mile back in high school and was in good shape just out of the potato field. I ran in step just behind him and did not realize until later that he was pissed off because I was pushing him. One day about 11:00 in the morning, he stopped the platoon from marching and asked if there was anyone in the platoon who thought he could out run him. I foolishly said, "I do, sir." He came near me and hit me in the gut so hard that I nearly passed out. That was his way of telling me to ease up, and I did. I always let a couple of guys behind him and ahead of me after that. I never liked him, but I had to respect what he wanted.

While at Parris Island, I was in platoon 201 and so was my cousin. He had arrived in an ambulance because of whatever happened to him when he was down in the doorway at the shed. I never did find out, but he was picked as the outstanding recruit in the platoon and got the Dress Blues Award at graduation. He was a tall guy and very neat. He could make up the neatest pack and was squared away as to be picked for that award. Marching came easy to him; he always looked good. He still had to serve four years and when I was out, he was still in the Marines. When he finally got out, he did exactly what he said he was going to do. As we traveled south on the train he told me he was going to take his old man for everything he could. He did do that and never amounted to anything.

As we went to the rifle range, I wound up qualifying as a sharpshooter with a score of 218. I never had any trouble after that while in boot camp. One thing that happened one night about one in the morning, a person in civilian clothing approached me as I was on my post. I challenged him to stop, but he did not. I was pretty sure that he was drunk. As he neared me, he grabbed my rifle from me, and I knew I needed to do something drastic. I tackled him and got my rifle back, and he stumbled away. While he was getting up, without calling, out I just swung my rifle letting him know what would happen if he tried again to take it. I reported the incident at the end of my shift and thought that would be the end of it. The next morning my drill instructor, Staff Sergeant Corey, called me into his office and told me to stand at ease. He started to ask me questions about the incident. I told him the truth, but I could tell he was not believing me. Finally, he asked me about the blood on my utility shirt. I looked down and knew that it was shoe polish. He then said, "Thank God for that." He told me that he would find out who did that to me, and he would make an example out of him for messing with one of his men. I found out several days later that it was a staff sergeant who worked in the mess hall, and my drill instructor beat him up and made sure he pointed him out to me.

I really liked that man and I know that he had part of his foot frozen off during the Korean War. One evening, as we were taken to a movie in boot camp, his family came in together, and they all sat down at the same time. It was not hard to tell that this was a true military family.

Dee sent me a letter every day, and sometimes I would get several at once. During mail call the drill instructor would call out my name, and as I went forward to pick it up, he would smell the perfume and make some comment.

Time passed quickly, and I graduated from Parris Island. Then I was on my way to Camp Geiger in North Carolina near Jacksonville. We were all to have about six weeks of infantry training, then I would go home for my first leave. On Sunday afternoons there was always a big horseshoe game going on, and each player would have to pay money if they wanted to play. It only took me a few minutes to know that I wanted to do that. For several weeks I would win 20 to 40 dollars. Then I would use that money to call Dee, and we would talk until the money was all gone.

I found out as I got my orders that my job in the Marine Corps was going to require me to go to school for more than six months in California at a naval communications center located just a couple miles north of Mexico. I was picked to prepare to work for the Naval Security Administration. That meant if I passed basic school, I would never be on a Marine Corps base again, and that I would work almost as a civilian but would still wear my uniform. My first assigned duty station was Imperial Beach. I was excited about the opportunity, and even more excited to get home to the girl that I already knew I wanted to be with me the rest of my life. I knew then that I would try to marry her, if she would have me.

A Full Life or Life of a Fool

Myself on active duty as a United States Marine in 1959.

The three weeks at home went by very quickly, perhaps because my Grandma Dellinger wanted to go to California to visit her oldest son and my mom's oldest brother. My Uncle Kenneth lived in Riverside perhaps 50 or 60 miles from the airport in Los Angeles. I was to make the trip to California with my grandma at my side and take her to meet my aunt and uncle before reporting to Imperial Beach. Bidding my family and the love of my life goodbye once again, my grandma (who was in her mid to late 80s) and I made our way onto a big TWA 747 jet and prepared to take off. This was Grandma's first flight, and I was a bit concerned how she would handle all of that. As the big jet roared down the runway and started to climb, I noticed it was climbing very quickly and really pulled us back in our seats. I will never forget my grandma's first words, "Wow, feel that power!" I thought it was a great statement from an elderly woman who had never before been in an airplane.

After saying good-bye to my grandma and aunt and Uncle Ken at the airport, I headed for Imperial Beach. I was there in basic and advanced school for nearly seven months. My sweetheart continued to write to me every day. Dee was about to finish her senior year in high school. We both wanted to marry and decided that we would do so. Breaking the news to my mom and dad would be the harder of the two. Her parents were older and Dee would be the second girl to leave the nest. The Godfrey family had accepted me very warmly, and I felt comfortable around her dad and mother.

I loved communication school and was quickly taught how to type and take code with earphones. The reason I was picked for this job was because of an aptitude test that had been given early on in boot camp. Do not ever think for one minute that the military does not know how to place people where they can excel at what comes naturally to them. There were just a few Marines but a lot of Navy men at this school. All the instructors were Navy. I never served under another Marine officer from that day on and until I left the Marine Corps.

Big Award at Imperial Beach, California.

There was an inspection once a month in that school that was conducted by the Navy. It was called the Honor Man Inspection. I decided that I would really try to win one of these inspections, so I started spit shining a pair of shoes every day. I left the shoe horn in the shoes so the buildup of polish would not crack but would get like a mirror that one could literally see himself reflected in those shoes.

Then came the appointed day of the inspection, and I carried those spit shined shoes with the shoe trees still in them to the place of the inspection. I slipped out the shoe trees and slipped my feet into the shoes. There was much talk about that, but I did win the inspection. I know it was because of the shine on those shoes and not because of my crossed eyes which did not make me look too sharp overall. The Naval inspector could not get past those spit-shined shoes. After the inspection was over and I walked back to the barracks, the shoes looked really bad. That polish cracked to pieces, and it took a while to get all that old polish off and start over.

During the first half of the time I spent going to school there, we were housed at a nearby naval air station. Every day we rode in big truck vans back and forth to school. Also while living there, I quickly got a job of setting bowling pins in the bowling alley at the base. I sent money home to put into my savings as I knew marriage was just around the corner.

We always had to go to a 6 P.M. and a 10 P.M. muster. The one at 6 was outside, and the one at 10 was inside a big barracks. One day, I had been setting pins and had to break away for a muster. There must have been 300 names called out, and because it was at a naval base it was run very loosely. I was a bit angry because it was so poorly done, and then some big Navy guy grabbed a Marine's cap. We called it a piss cutter cap because of its shape and it had a Marine Corps emblem on it. This Navy guy grabbed this cover and threw it. He was supposed to be at attention, and this cover hit me in the eye. At this time, I had a sty on my eye. I got mad and yelled at this guy who was acting up, and he promptly hit me in the mouth with his fist and split my lip wide open. I had to go to the base hospital and have my lip stitched. I bled like a stuck pig, and it took seven stitches inside and seven outside to fix it. As I returned to my barracks to take a shower, I noticed that I had blood all over my uniform and that was a problem. I was also told by my buddies in my barracks that this guy had a big ring on his hand when he hit me. It was nearly time for the 10 P.M. muster. I put that bloody uniform back on and went up to the barracks where the muster was to be held. That guy was housed in that building. When he saw me approaching, and as I got to his bunk (even though I knew it was the same guy), I asked him if he was the one who hit me earlier.

He replied, "Hell yes, and what about it?" He took off that big ring and threw it on his bunk. This guy was at least six inches taller than I was. I immediately flew into him, and a short time later I was pulled off of him by some guys who believed that I was going to kill him. We had upset quite a few lockers, and when it was all over, I do not think he ever hit me, or hardly at all. My now swelled-up lip was not bleeding, and I felt a lot better. It was most likely a good thing that we were separated because I would not have quit until he was totally subdued. There was no telling how much trouble I would have gotten in, and at the time, I did not care. The muster had not yet begun so nothing official ever happened. When I saw him in a later muster, he definitely looked worse than I did.

Later on at Imperial Beach when we were on the main base instead of the naval air station, some unique things happened. Bill Steyer, a Marine friend of mine from Nebraska, and I decided to go to the San Diego Track at Balboa Park to a car race. We got seats in the first row. As the main event was about to begin, they announced the drivers and gave special recognition to this one guy who was a US Navy veteran. He was now running a service station in San Diego and they asked people to patronize him for their car repairs.

We suddenly realized that his wife and three young daughters were sitting two rows directly behind us. On the second lap that veteran's car flipped. It came to rest on its top, and having a seat belt on, the driver seemed to be unhurt but was struggling to get out of the seat belt. He was just hanging there. His car was only about 20 feet from where we were sitting. Suddenly, there appeared a flicker of flame under the front of the car and very quickly the whole car was enveloped with fire. Several men with fire gear tried to put the fire out. The driver screamed twice, and we knew he was gone. They canceled the race, and Bill and I walked speechlessly for several miles. That was a very bad evening, and one we would never forget.

On the lighter side, I remember Bill used to fake throwing epileptic fits, falling down stairs while just faking it and not getting hurt. We had a bunch of new people and we were on the second floor. Taps played at 11 P.M. The lights went out on the main bay on our floor, and Bill said to me, "Hey, Willy (as he called me), it is time for a fit." He immediately pulled himself into position in order to roll down the stairs. The only problem was just as he hit the bottom and people had come running, he rolled right into the legs of the Officer of the Day who had chosen to visit our barracks that evening as Taps was played. The unsuspecting officer called for an ambulance, and they carted Bill off to the hospital. Three days later, Bill returned and that was the end of the demonstrations. He said he thought he was going to be put out of the service for medical reasons, but he did not want to tell them that he was just faking it. He was not sure what would have been the worst medicine to swallow.

    Because of working as much as I could to earn extra money to send home, I had not been south into Mexico yet. The guys kept telling me that I just had to go. I asked them how much I had to spend to do that, and they told me that the bus ticket down cost 50 cents and the bus ticket back was 50 cents. Also needed, was 50 cents for a beer and then another 50 cents for that woman that picked a guy up when entering the bar. Also needed was ten dollars for the pimp for the service of the woman. I thought to myself that I did not want any whore, so I would only take $2, and that is what I did without telling anybody. As we got off the bus and walked down the street, I saw we were heading to the Tiviley Club. When we got there we had to slide down a sliding board into the basement where we were each grabbed by our private parts by a woman and took off to a booth. Next, two beers were delivered to us and I had to use up all my money except the 50 cents needed to ride back to the base. I did not drink so I gave the beer to the girl that was with me. There was a raised boxing ring in the center of this building and lots of loud music playing with much yelling and cheering. There were naked women on the stage and men and women doing things that I would never have been able to explain to my dad. Now I had another problem. I did not speak Spanish, but I did understand what this woman was saying had to do with me having sex with her for 10 "bucky," which I did understand. I finally convinced her to drink the beer that was intended for me, and while she was drinking, I looked around to see how I could get out of this place. I quickly decided that I needed to get to the stairway which had a door at the top. Guys and girls were going up, and I somehow convinced her to take me to that door before she would get 10 bucks from me. I should have known that this so called pimp would be somewhere collecting money. The woman was to already have the 10 bucks from me before she got that far and was to give it to him. As we eased our way up the stairs to the pimp at the top, he started having a conversation with the woman. I saw the door that led out of the club. I did not hesitate, and as I walked swiftly past many guys having sex sideways on several couches that were lined up end to end, I never looked back. As I got outside, I broke into a run expecting a knife to go into my back at any time. I made it several blocks before I slowed my pace and started looking for a bus. I still had 50 cents to get out of this hell hole and get back to the base. I burned that last 50 cents with the bus driver and felt better after arriving back at the base. Because I was sober, I shall never forget that experience. What has really stuck with me over the years is the foul odor that was in that room with the couches and all that activity. I can tell you that night before I closed my eyes and went to sleep, that I thanked God for his protection. I just knew that could have been a fatal night for an American serviceman in Mexico. I really just blamed myself for the whole issue.

I continued to play horseshoes and would always use any money that I won to call home and talk to my Dee back in Pennsylvania. She continued to write me every day, and I was really in love with this girl. I decided to formally ask her to marry me when I returned home for Christmas. One way or another, we would marry as soon as possible. The only problem was that I knew my parents would be very upset. They thought we were too young. I did respect my parents, but I had reached the time in my life when I was going to do what I wanted to do. There would be no fighting with us from Dee's parents as they were much older and happy with the guy she had picked to marry. Now all we had to do was break the news to my parents.

Just before I left Imperial Beach, my orders for my next duty station arrived. Those orders would take me to the Philippines and to the base known as San Miguel. This seemed to set up the perfect situation as I had saved enough money to get Dee over to the Philippines and get married and live with me over there. We would return married, and that is what this nineteen-year-old had all figured out. I came home on leave, and we both felt good about what we were about to do.

Then came the setback. After being home for nearly 30 days, I got on a plane to Treasure Island, San Francisco. I quickly learned from other servicemen that were coming back from the Far East that it was not possible to keep a wife from America who got married in the Philippines, but she would have to return to the States and apply to go back to the Philippines as a dependent. I did not have enough money to accomplish all of that, so then I did have a new problem.

New Life 6:

Husband and Wife

When I found out that Dee and I would have to marry before I went to Luzon Island in order for her to live with me while I was there, I was devastated. I had been trained in boot camp to obey orders without question, and I accepted that. However, I could not accept the fact that Dee and I would be separated the first two years of our married life, and there was no war going on at the time. I was maturing, and decided that one way or another, even if I had to go back to Pennsylvania to marry her before my ship left, I would do so at all costs. The next day I went to the Commanding Office at Treasure Island, San Francisco, California, and pleaded my case.

I tried to be respectful and yet firm in my resolve. Keep in mind, I had just come off 30 days of leave and was scheduled to ship out to Luzon 15 days from that day. I explained my situation to the best of my ability and hoped for a good result. The officer stated to me that this was not a valid request, and I could see it was going nowhere. I very quickly said, "Sir, if you do not grant my request, I will just leave here, go back to Pennsylvania, get married, return here before the ship leaves, and take my punishment." The officer said, "Wilson, I believe you are serious, and I am going to grant you seven days leave, and you better be back here on time or your ass will fry!" I calmly said, "Thank you, Sir; I will be back on time."

I had to do some quick planning. First, I called Dee and explained the situation to her, telling her that we could get married next Thursday. She said that she would make the arrangements. I told her to call the minister at my church and ask if we could use the church hall for the reception. I am in San Francisco and have one week to get home for my wedding. Then I have less than a week to get back to the base after the wedding.

I found out that I could get a cab over to the Oakland Naval Air Station and try to get a HOP or a free flight towards Pennsylvania. I found out that there was a flight to Corpus Christi, Texas, leaving in a few hours, and by this time it was Thursday evening. So I took the flight and suddenly realized that I needed to call home and explain to my folks what was happening.

When I got my mother on the phone and told her that Dee and I would be married on Thursday of next week, she quickly said, "We will see about that." I calmly and seriously told her that if she wanted to be there she would see the wedding. I did not hang up, but rather assured her that Dee would take care of the details.

I got on the plane with a bunch of naval officers, and we took off for Texas. After landing in the middle of the night, I found another flight heading to Norfolk, Virginia, about daylight on Friday. I soon learned that this flight only had crew members on it. It was only part of a crew, so I was allowed to sit in a crew member's seat. I had microphones on my head and could hear all the flight chatter. The wind was blowing up a small storm as we took off. This was a seaplane, so it was pretty rough as we took off, but I did not mind it because I did not know any better having never been on a seaplane before this time. Shortly after takeoff, I heard a voice on my head set requesting an emergency landing. I was thinking to myself that someone must be in trouble, only to find out it was my pilot making the request. I was smelling fuel in the plane, but that did not upset me at first because I was a farm kid and used to the smell of gasoline. The smell had grown stronger and the plane was bumping around. The next thing I knew, one of the co-pilots was checking my shoes for cleats. He explained to me that someone, while fueling up the plane before takeoff, had run gallons of fuel that were not in the tank but in the bottom of the plane and was sloshing around. About that time, I heard the other co-pilot saying on the radio that he was setting the plane on a course to ditch it so many miles off the Florida coast, and then going on radio silence and leaving the cockpit. I began to realize the seriousness of the situation, and the fumes were now very strong. A few minutes later, I had a parachute strapped onto me, which was a totally new experience. All the hatches in the plane had been opened. I was instructed to put one foot out the hatch onto the outside step and prepare to jump if the Lieutenant JG pushed me. He told me that we might get far enough away from the plane before it blew. He further told me that if one spark ignited we would be in trouble, and that is why he had checked my shoes for steel cleats.

We flew for some time that way, and the smell did lessen because of all the hatches being open. This was the middle of January, and even in the South it was very cold as the air blew in and out of the plane. I think there were only three others on board beside myself and the co-pilots. A Navy first class petty officer took off his parachute and volunteered to crawl down into the belly of the plane with a plastic bucket and a big sponge. When he was done sopping up the gasoline, he had four or five 5-gallon buckets that were almost full. They decided to siphon it out of the plane. The guy that sucked up the gas to get it started got sick from the gasoline, as he most likely swallowed some of it in the process. As I stood over in the hatch ready to jump, daylight appeared and I could see the ground below me. Even though I had never jumped from a plane, I was not afraid to jump; although, I could only think of landing in quicksand and sinking into the swampy ground below me. The thought of not being able to get home to my wedding was looming in my mind as the minutes rolled. About an hour later, the smell had become a lot less. The one co-pilot went back to flying the plane and we flew all the way to Norfolk on radio silence. We finally landed without knowing for sure where we were. When we hit the water, the pilot cut the engine and told me to sit still until they would come and tow us into port. We were safe, and for several hours had much conversation about our being glad to be alive and well. After several hours, a couple of boats came and towed us into the base. The two co-pilots lived in Arlington, Virginia, with their wives and families. They were getting a ticket on a commercial airline to fly to Washington, D.C., and taking a cab home from there. They invited me to travel with them to the commercial airport in Norfolk, and I could buy a ticket on the same plane to Washington and then get a taxi to my home some 60 miles to the north in Pennsylvania. Those two guys bought round trip tickets because they were going home for the weekend and returning on Sunday to Norfolk. I just bought a one-way ticket to Washington. I thanked both of them, and they wished me well and said our good-byes. I felt that I was doing pretty good because I had gotten from San Francisco to nearly home by the way of Texas in just over a day. In the late hours of Friday, I got back to Dallastown, Pennsylvania, and my soon-to-be wife. I was so young and excited that I was not even tired—just ready to start a new phase in my life. We talked into the night, and Dee had things pretty well lined up for the wedding. We planned a real short honeymoon as I had to make it back to the base in Treasure Island on time.

On Monday, I heard some stunningly bad news as a Capital Air Lines Viscount plane with some thirty people on board had crashed between Washington and Norfolk killing all on board. My two friends who helped me get home were on that plane as it returned from Chicago. I am still amazed at how one near accident was followed up by a fatal accident. It was so sad, and I still often think about it.

Our wedding night came quickly and all went well. Two families who could have met some 19 years earlier in the York Hospital baby ward were now witnessing the marriage of those two kids. After our one-day honeymoon, I had to prepare to get back to Treasure Island in order to catch the ship to Luzon. I did not have any reservations about flying, even though I had that bad experience coming home and then hearing about the deaths of my two short term friends. I had many thoughts and prayers for their families.

I was sad to leave my new wife, but the thought of being reunited soon was what kept me going. I returned in plenty of time, so nothing was said about the extra leave as I prepared for the long boat trip to Luzon in the Philippines. I never much liked the water or boats, and I had never been on a big ship like this one. As I looked down at the dock and saw the ship moving up and down and in and out against the pier, I started to feel a bit queasy. I knew before we had gone one mile in the bay that I was going to throw up. I think that I had the flu, but, for sure, I was a sick pup. That lasted for 19 days as that was how long I was on the ship. I lost a lot of weight and was so weak that I had trouble carrying my sea bag off the ship which I was required to do.

We were put on a bus and traveled to San Miguel, a base in Northwestern Luzon near the town of San Antonio. Arriving in the middle of the night, we were ushered into a barracks and told to pick a bunk. I picked a top bunk, crawled in, and went to sleep only to be awakened by lights on in the barracks and a couple of corpsmen (these were the Navy medics) yelling for us to roll out and get on our feet and skin her back. I asked a guy in the next rack what

A Full Life or Life of a Fool

was going on, and he said it was a pecker check. Apparently, there was a venereal disease problem, and this was a somewhat routine check to keep things under control. To me, a newly married Marine, this was bullshit. I just plain refused to do it. After someone explained that I just arrived this morning, they quit trying to get me out of my rack.

We were immediately put to work. We rode in a big van out to the communications shack which was about two miles from the barracks. The work we did was very secret, and everything at that base was closely guarded. So I began the job that I had been trained to do. Every day from then on, I worked for the Marine Corps in that building. My shift was from 6 P.M. until 12 P.M., and then 6 A.M. until 6 P.M., and then 12 P.M. until 6 A.M. Then I had three and a half days off. All of this was during a five-day week. Each time, I went back to work two days earlier in the week than the week before. It was great duty, and it proved to be even greater as my wife was about to come and join me.

I began immediately to obtain permission to have my wife join me. However, I quickly found out that I would have to live near Olongapole. That was about 40K away from where I would be stationed. No problem; I bought a Lambretta motor scooter and started looking for a place for us to live. I found a small development of houses built by the Navy Seabees during the war with Japan. They were plain but nice enough for me and my new bride.

New Life 7:

Together Again

Dee got all of her shots, and we purchased an airline ticket to Manilla by way of Los Angeles and several stops at islands in the Pacific. I, of course, had no leave, so I had to get the precise time for me to leave my base and pick up Dee. All went well, and by the time she got there I was at Manilla ready to pick her up. We traveled to our old "new house," and I was so proud to have picked this house for Dee and me.

Although she never complained about the fact that there were no curtains or blinds (looking back on it), I do not think she thought it was as great a house as I did. I had to return to work the next day for two days totally away from her. Meanwhile, she had found a ride to the base store, bought some material, and by the time I got home again, she had made new curtains and had them hung. Things looked like a home now, and she had done all that in just two days!

There were several families that lived next to us. Of course, they were military, and Dee now had a circle of friends in just a few days' time. There was a mountain at one side of our house, and we would hike up there and take pictures of our house below, enjoying the beautiful scenery.

The base at Subic Bay was about one mile from our house, and rides were available by Jeep for just a dime. The Jeeps were all beat up and driven by young native men. It was common for them to rub fenders with one another as they fought for customers. Half way to the base was a gas station that was selling Caltex gasoline. It had the same star as a Texaco station in the states.

The Olongapool River ran through the town, and people fished off of the bridge going across the river. Just outside of Klackan Heights (which was the name of our development) was a cockpit stadium. This provided a place for gambling and watching roosters fighting to the death. I only went once to see what occurred. It was very loud and a bit frightening as many of the people seemed to be quite angry. Not speaking the language made me a bit uncomfortable, so I did not go back again. There was no admission price, so anyone could watch for free.

Sometimes we would go with our friends who had a car to Manga Beach which was three or four kilometers from our house. The water was beautiful, and we had so much fun as we ate our packed lunch and just loved life. Two of our closest friends were Bruce and Dianne Johnson from Wisconsin. They were Navy people, and Bruce worked at Subic Bay, and he was the one who owned the car. One day we were at Manga Beach with no one else around. The girls were sunning themselves on the beach, and Bruce and I were out in the water about 60 yards from the beach. The water was crystal clear and about 4 to 5 feet deep. I thought Bruce was off to my left about 20 feet, and I just knew I saw him underwater. But as I glanced at the beach, I realized that he had gone up to the beach and was walking towards the girls. I quickly realized that what I thought was Bruce was actually a big barracuda. It was very difficult to walk swiftly when I was in water up to my eyes, but I moved as fast as I could, trying not to attract that barracuda. Later that same week, we noticed in the Star Newspaper, the Far Eastern military paper that was available at the base each week, that a native had been killed by a barracuda near the base at Subic Bay. That spot was less than four kilometers from where we were on the beach. That was our last trip to that beach.

We used to sit outside the base on the way up the hill to Cubic Point Naval Hospital and watch the planes take off and land on different aircraft carriers. This was so much fun to watch, and I never grew tired of doing that. Cubic Point Naval Hospital proved to be the birthplace of our first child, and she would have both Philippine and American citizenship until her eighteenth birthday. When I took Dee to the hospital, the nurses kicked me out and said I was not needed there. They told me to go bowling and come back later. No longer would that be told to the father-to-be. It was not a problem, and when I returned our little daughter Kimberly Ann and her mother were just fine.

We got a new house girl who stayed with Dee and Kim to help out with the washing and cleaning of the house. Her name was Lena, and we loved her like a daughter as she was so much help and so much fun. Lena's dad owned a farm, and one day we rented a taxi and drove about 45 kilometers to the farm and spent part of the day with her parents. They were plowing the soil in one of the fields with an ox, which is the beast of burden in the Philippines. It was a one bottom plow, and they permitted me to drive the ox which thrilled me to death as I was now in the environment that I loved and cherished. I expected to someday soon be doing this for myself and my family, but not with an ox! Some would refer to it as a water buffalo. There were many of these animals on the island, and it was not a good thing to harm one in any way. While driving a car, people had to be aware that the oxen had the right of way.

Plowing in the Philippines with an ox and a one bottom plow.

We took a trip to Baguio City which was up in the mountains. We rented a taxi and driver for that trip. We traveled about 200 miles up and back, and I got to know the driver. He was a very interesting person to talk to as he was a teenager when the Japanese took over the island of Luzon. He told me a story of how he and his friends rescued a shot down American pilot, tearing the radio out of his plane so as to be able to call for help. About two days later, a submarine came into Subic Bay and picked him up. They had helped the pilot get away without the Japs catching him. We took many pictures that day and still have them. We really loved the Philippines and had so much fun in the nearly two years that we were there.

I decided to take about six days off and fly to Hong Kong to have some clothing made for Dee and to buy some shoes and gifts to send home for Christmas. The military plane on which I flew was a transport plane with mostly officers on board. The pilot who was also going to stay in Hong Kong, warned us not to bring back more than 96 pounds of stuff. I obeyed perfectly, weighing all that I had bought. When I got on board with my gear, I could not believe all the stuff that was there. As the pilot, who was drunk at the time, entered the plane, he screamed, cursed, and stumbled through the gear that was not stowed properly because it was more than all the straps could have tied fast.

Being sober, I did not have a good feeling about this and wondered what might happen. Would I, as an enlisted man, have to give up some of my purchased goods, even though they weighed less than 96 pounds? The next thing I knew, I heard the planes' engines starting up and we were taking off. Hong Kong is down in behind some mountains and kind of in a hole, so trying to get enough elevation to fly out was not easy. We must have circled around that airport for more than 20 minutes before we went on our way. The engines were groaning under a full load, and I think even yet, if one engine had sputtered we would have crashed into the harbor below us.

When we started housekeeping in Luzon, we had driven in a rented vehicle to Clark Air Force Base in order to buy a stove and refrigerator. Now, as we were preparing to leave the Philippines, we needed to sell those appliances. I soon found out that there was no legal way for us to do that. All we could do was sell it on the black market to some dealer. I feared getting caught and decided to go to a place where I heard that they bought a lot of stuff. As I sat and listened to a conversation with the executive officer of the Subic Bay

A Full Life or Life of a Fool

Base making a deal with this Philippine lady buyer, I felt a bit better about what I was doing. But after I did my deal, I knew that I would not feel good about it until our ship set sail for California.

Knowing that I would be discharged shortly after reaching Treasure Island, I took the advantage of buying a car to be delivered to me at Treasure Island as I arrived on the ship. I bought a 1955 Ford, and all went smoothly as had been promised. I was permitted to stay topside with my wife and little girl on the trip home, and I was thankful for that. Dee's mother had flown out to Los Angeles to meet her nephew and Dee's cousin who lived in the part of LA known as Eagle Rock. While in the dining room on the ship, the Philippine butler, chefs, and waiters loved our little girl Kim. They carried her around while we were eating, and she loved the attention they were giving her. To this very day she is quick to befriend any warm-blooded person or animal, and I firmly believe that this was a result of all the attention she got from the Philippine people in her early life.

Our new family in the Philippines; daughter Kimberly.

As we docked for a very short visit in Honolulu and got off the ship, we sat on a small wall with some sand behind us enjoying the sunshine and beautiful landscape. Dee had just changed a very stinky diaper and asked me, "What can we do with this?" Being a farm boy and having noticed more than once a cat making a crap in the wheat bin, digging a hole and covering it up, I responded without any hesitation; I dug a hole in the sand and finished the job. There really was no other place to put that dirty diaper that I could see, and we had to get back on the ship very soon.

This is in Hawaii where a dirty diaper had to be buried.

As we sailed into the dock at Treasure Island, Dee's mother and cousin were waiting down below. This was the first look at her new granddaughter for Meda Godfrey. The plan was for Dee and Kim to travel to LA and stay until I was discharged. Then I would drive my '55 Ford to LA, and we would travel to Pennsylvania by way of Phoenix, Arizona, stopping to see my uncle who had bought the TV set for his sister and my grandparents some years ago. Because of what I knew about him, I wanted to see him in person and spend a couple of days with him before I headed to PA, to begin my life there as head of my family.

My 1955 car was an oil hog. A tank of gas had to accompany at least four quarts of oil. Because my uncle owned a Texaco service station, I would only burn Texaco gas. I could tell anyone that I left a string of quart oil cans across the USA. I knew then that what had seemed like a good deal was not going to be a good deal in the end. I could only hope that we would make it home. I did not share those concerns with Dee, but they were on my mind every time I opened another can of oil and dumped it into that Ford.

This is the '55 Ford that I bought in the Philippines to be delivered in California. In Phoenix, I found out why he and his estranged sister (who happened to be my grandmother) did not get along. Walter Bartol, my great uncle, was a bit on the rough side but fun to be around. Uncle Walter had gone out West as a young man and worked in the livery stable in Phoenix before World War I. During this time period, the West was truly wild, and there was not much law and order. After the war, he took his pension from the government and bought that livery stable.

My uncle Walter Bartol at his ranch in Phoenix in 1961.

From that time on, his business practices allowed him to be involved in building Phoenix by buying and owning most of what is now Greater Phoenix. His son owned and operated a big ranch southwest of Phoenix. Walter owned many service stations, and he took me to a place where he said he would eventually be when he died. He was now in his early 80s. He took us to the Elks' Club, of which he was a member, for supper and showed us a very nice time. He wanted me to stay and go mountain lion hunting with him on his ranch in Flagstaff. But as much as I wanted to do that, I felt the obligation to get my family back to Pennsylvania more. He would soon sell his ranch in Phoenix for high rise buildings to be built because the pressure was pushing him out. He lived for several more years, and before he died, the city of Phoenix did many hours of tape about his life which is now part of the Archives of Phoenix. Unbeknownst to me, I would return to Phoenix later in life with my wife and my parents to visit Uncle Walter's son who was Walter Junior. He is the one that owned the ranch in Southwest Phoenix when this visit occurred. Before I continue with the details of the trip to Pa., I will say that Walter Bartol played a very important part in my future life. However, I would not realize this until I returned to Phoenix when I was nearly 60 years old. Going as fast as possible, we made the trip home safely in that oil-crazed Ford.

As we arrived home, we visited the Godfrey residence and found my family and Pappy Godfrey waiting in the living room for the reunion. This was their first look at our little Kim who was a cute one-year old plus a couple of weeks. The biggest shock for me was that my little sister Gloria, of whom I had not seen much since I went off to the Marine Corps when she was only eight, had grown into a pretty young lady. When I saw her, my first thought was that something bad had happened to her, and they had gotten a replacement for her to save me from the shock. That feeling did not last long, but I shall never forget it.

As we talked that evening, I grabbed a newspaper and started looking for ads for help wanted. The next morning, I went to Quality & Service Dairy to answer one of the ads. It was a Saturday morning, and the owner Glenn Cooper interviewed me and asked me when I would be ready to start. I told him that today would be fine, and he laughed and told me to come in Monday and that I was hired.

One of the questions that he asked me was what my intentions were as far as a career was concerned, and I told him that I would work for him until I could buy a farm and become a farmer. Some years later, he told me that he thought to himself that I had just gotten out of the Marines and would be a route man for him for a long time. Less than two years later, I left him to become a farmer.

My milk truck as parked at my house in Dallastown.

Now that I had a job, I had to find a place for us to live. Dee's mom told us that we could stay with them, and so we did until I found a place a few days later. We rented a place on Main Street in Dallastown, just a block from her parents and only one mile from the dairy where I was to be employed.

My wife's parents Roy and Meda Godfrey in 1968.

October had arrived and the mornings waxed colder. My oil guzzling Ford was threatening to not start, and I could see trouble coming. I did not ever want to be late for any job that I had. This car was losing compression, so I traded it on a new 1962 Chevy four cylinder. Of course, I had to finance it because money was on the low side. Now we have a child, a rented home, a new car, and a job which paid $75 a week delivering milk. Mr. Cooper told me that the milk route had potential but needed work. He promised me that when the commissions on that route were consistently over $75 per week, he would put me on commission so I would have a chance to reap the benefits of my work. By February of 1963, I was put on commission bringing in about $105 per week. I quickly paid off my car. An elderly lady used to sell plants and flowers at a stand in front of the place we were renting. So I figured that if we could continue that without interruption, we should be able to make some extra money. Dee could tend the stand. I got hooked up with Millers Plant Farm, and we did very well that spring.

My milk route was in York, PA, on Monday, Wednesday, and Friday. I went north of the city on Tuesday, Thursday, and Saturday. I loaded my truck about 3:30 A.M. and would get back past my house around 1 P.M. Some days I would stop and drop off some milk for us, and I would even catch a short nap before going the last mile to the dairy to unload my truck and turn in my order for the next day. I did not work by the hour, and I knew I would have to wait to get up to the dock, so I would just spend a little more time at my house.

One day Mr. Cooper or Glenn as I now called him, told the lady in the office that when I was finished unloading, he wanted to talk to me. That was the first time but not the last time that he did that. I did not give much thought as to what he might want to talk to me about. So I entered his office, and sat down. He had a habit of wearing his glasses down on his nose which I thought looked dumb. He proceeded to tell me that he had gotten a call from a lady in Dallastown who assured him that one of his milkmen was seeing a lady and spending too much time there for any good to be coming of it. I asked him what part of Dallastown, and he said East Main Street. Well, I lived on East Main Street, and I knew that he knew that. Seeing that I was about to get pissed off, he started laughing and told me I needed to go across the street to my neighbor Mrs. Shaffer and introduce myself to her. I calmly told him that I would take care of that in about ten minutes. Mr. Cooper thought it was really funny, but I did not appreciate it one little bit. As I got home, I realized

A Full Life or Life of a Fool

that she could not see me leaving the truck because the truck blocked her view. So I went out the side door of the truck and went into my house.

I talked to Dee and told her what Mr. Cooper said and what I was now going to do. I walked across the street and knocked on Mrs. Shaffer's door. I told her to take a good look at me, and she did. I asked her, "Do you know who I am?" She said, "Why, yes, you are Mr. Wilson from across the street." I then asked her, "What do you think I do for a living?" She said that she had no idea. I replied that I was a milkman for Quality and Service Diary." She replied, "O my God! I am so sorry," realizing what she had done. I told her that I had a garden in the back of my house, and it needed to be spaded in order to plant. I had a shovel in the little shack by the garden, and if she did not have enough to do she could come over and spade my garden. I turned around and went back to my house across the street. In the spring, I felt bad about what I had said to her, so I took her two boxes of nice strawberries from my father's farm. We later became friends, and she and her husband came to visit my wife and me on the farm that we bought several years later.

While working for Mr. Cooper at this first job, I had some unusual things happen. One very foggy morning, I came in to load my truck and found Bob Markle not able to get his truck started. He asked me to get the big ice truck and give him a pull. He would get the tow chain, and I could back up to his truck. The ice truck had just little mirrors on it, and it was a big covered box used to haul ice from the ice plant. It was parked alongside the repair garage which was on a bit of a hill that sloped down to where all the trucks were parked. Behind the ice truck was a two-wheel travel trailer that Mr. Cooper used for his vacations. As I pulled the truck away from the garage and positioned it to back up to Bob's milk truck, he kept yelling to come on back and indicated that it was a long way from being near his truck. Bob thought I was backing too slowly, so he ran to get a chain thinking he had plenty of time to get it and still give me directions. I thought he was angry because I was backing too slowly. It was really foggy, and I could see nothing. I counted on Bob to tell me when to stop so I would not hit his truck. However, I sped up too much and backed into his milk truck, pushing the radiator into the motor. Bob yelled too late to stop me. He told me to just put the ice truck away, and he would use old #13, which was a spare truck if needed early in the morning. I was upset because I knew that I was going to catch hell from Mr. Cooper. So I am backing the ice truck into place and I suddenly realized that I hit the cement garage with the back right hand corner of the ice truck. I stopped, pulled up, and straightened out so the truck would be next to the garage. But as I stopped, I realized that I had now hit Mr. Cooper's trailer. The blocks in front of the wheels that were to keep it from rolling down this hill were gone. As I shut the truck off after pulling it a foot forward, I saw the trailer rolling down over the hill and heading for truck #13 that Bob was going to take. The trailer finally came to rest against #13, and Bob said, "Get the hell out of here before you ruin anything else!" I jumped into my truck and thought throughout the day that this would be the end of my job. As I returned to the dairy to unload, once again Mr. Cooper wanted to see me in his office. His glasses were down on his nose and he said, "I have just one thing to say to you." (I thought he would fire me). But he blurted out the following, "The next time someone asks you for help here in the morning, you tell them to go to hell, and get in your truck and get out of here. Do you understand?" I said, "Yes, Sir." I was very relieved that I did not have to tell Dee that I got fired.

Sometime later, all the drivers were given a letter that a nighttime sales meeting was to be held and all drivers must be present. That meeting although not attended by Mr. Cooper, was run by a high pressure salesman from the Dale Carnegie School of Selling. As the meeting continued, we were told that we would be taking an eight week course on selling. We would each be billed half of the costs and the dairy would pay the other half. After the school was over there would be a contest which would allow us to earn back the half that we had to pay. I did not like this guy because of his high pressure tactics. At the end of the evening, we were to sign to take the course, and I was the only one who refused to sign. When asked if I wanted to keep my job working for the dairy, I bluntly told him that I did. But if it came down to my taking the course or not, I would find another job. I was angry.

The next day, Mr. Cooper wanted to talk to me again. He offered to pay both halves up front for me, and he wanted me to sign up for the course. I thought about this for a little while and then told him that if I had to sell milk like this man tried to sell this school to us last night, I would hate my job and find another. He asked me, "Do you not believe that this school will make you a better milkman?" I told him that I would not sign to take this course under any circumstances. However, I did tell him that if he had the contest on selling milk, and if I did not win, I would pay all the costs of the school, and I would go and do it.

A Full Life or Life of a Fool

He explained that we were going to have a new product called Guernsey Royal. It would sell for one penny per quart more. The contest would last for 10 weeks and would pit each driver against the other to see who would get the most done the quickest. He said, "Wilson, I will have this contest started next week, and I will take you up on your offer." There were 15 routes, and when he put up this big chart on the wall at the dairy, I knew that I had better win, or I would be the laughing stock of the dairy.

I was a workaholic. The chart was made with 15 red lines running along the line across the wall of the office. By the end of the second week, my line was over halfway to the goal. No other line had gotten past the goal of the second week. By the end of the third week my line was near the goal for nine weeks. No one else had made it past the fourth week. Sometime during the following week, the whole chart was torn down, and I never heard one word of praise. Even though it took a few weeks for the rest of the men to warm up to me, by the end of a month all had returned to normal. I sold more of the Guernsey Royal milk than any other route driver, and that continued until the day I left the dairy, which came more quickly than I realized.

I remember the first winter as I delivered on Maryland Avenue in York. It was a cold morning, and it had rained the night before and black ice was everywhere. The streets were not too bad, but the sidewalks and edges of porches were slick. In that part of York there were a lot of second and third floor apartments. Usually couples just starting out, lived in those. These were potentially good customers, but during this time of their lives they perhaps both worked and did not order but one quart of milk per delivery. I had to march up the outside fire escape to a back door in the apartment on a sheet metal porch. That particular morning as I fought my way up those stairs with a quart of milk, I neared the top and noticed an empty milk bottle between the screen door and the other door with a note in the top. Fighting to keep from falling, I got my flashlight out and braced my foot against the top post on the little porch. I read the following, "Milkman, please, no milk today, but leave a quarter pound of butter." As I fought my way down the steps with the quart of milk that was not needed, walked to the truck and got the butter, then walked back up the steps to the icy porch, I had this piercing thought going through my mind. The commission on butter was one cent per pound, and I just made two trips up and down for one-fourth of a cent. I was saying in my mind, "Boy, you better find a better way to make a living than this." Farming now became even more appealing to me.

I heard of several farms for sale, and my dad and I checked them out. One was too small to make a living on it. The one that I wanted to buy was owned by a widow who wanted to sell. I went to see her, and she told me that I would need more money to buy her farm than I could get, and I should face the fact that I would not be able to buy it. I had already been to the bank and was told that I would need at least 20% down. I tried, unsuccessfully, to explain that farm prices were rising faster than the money I was making at the dairy. I would never be able to get started with that requirement. This was a big disappointment, but it did not dampen my desire. The word was "out" in the community that I wanted a farm. In the spring of 1962, while my seventeen-year-old brother was at the feed mill picking up some supplies for my dad, one of the guys at the mill told him that his sister had a farm for sale and that he should tell his brother to go talk to her. Would this be the break for which I was looking?

New Life 8:

The Beginning of My Dream

I knew that my dad was very skeptical about my starting to farm because it was kind of tough to get started. It was hard work for what was achieved. I sort of dismissed the idea that my dad had due to the fact that he was older now. He would not want to go through the start up again since he had it a bit more comfortable now than his memories of how it was when he attempted to do the very same thing. I knew that my wife would support whatever I did, especially now as our second child was on the way. Most of all, because of some unknown reason at that time, I was driven with a passion to farm. No matter what came of it, it would be better than climbing icy steps to have to return to the customer with a quarter pound of butter!

I used to go down to my parents' place most every weekend. My brother reported to me on one of those trips that I should go out and talk to Mrs. Reherd who was the sister of Fulton McDonald. Fulton worked at the feed mill where Dad dealt. I drove out there within 15 minutes, wondering if this would bear any fruit. I did not believe that I had ever been on that road. Arriving, I noticed a big, red barn freshly painted and a nice sized house, not so freshly painted. Mrs. Reherd answered the door and welcomed me. I noticed that she was well-weathered by the sun and had the strong arms of a hard worker. I quickly told her why I was there, and she said that she was expecting me. That kind of shocked me as I had never seen this woman before this time. She went on to explain that her husband Raymond had recently died after some tough years of being ill. It was obvious that she had been working extremely hard and this was, most likely, taking its toll on her appearance. I learned later that she was not a well-groomed woman to begin with, but that was no indication that she was not a bright, independent, quality human being who had a big heart, good head for business, and was outspoken to go along with all of her other quality traits. I would quickly learn how much she would influence and shape this new part of my life and my family's future.

Mrs. Reherd—or Catherine, as I was told to address her—explained that she and her husband had no children. She felt it was now necessary to leave the farm. The next farm up the road was where she grew up with her brother (who had married later in life), and he owned that farm. The four of them had worked the farms together since they joined one another. Now I realized that her brother's wife was my fifth grade teacher and she was still teaching at this time. Catherine continued to explain that their farm had been in the Soil Bank, a government program for farmers who did not want to plant crops but to just keep the land free of weeds. It was kind of like she was apologizing to me because the farm did not look better. I had not even looked at the farm because I came up the road from New Park and did not even realize what fields belonged to her farm.

So now was my opportunity to share with her that my desire to farm was great, but my experience of trying to purchase a farm had not been successful thus far. I told her that I had tried to buy a nice farm about 5 miles from her place, but the lady turned me down. I explained that I had no money and could not borrow from the bank unless I had 20% to put down. We talked about my being a milk delivery man and that I had a wife and two children to support. Our son Bryan had recently been born. She encouraged me by saying that there should be a way for her to sell her farm to me. She did not have to have all the money at once. She would allow me to pay her so much each year after I sold my crops, and then I would pay her interest on the amount that I would still owe. She further stated that if I knew someone who could help us figure out how to do this, I should bring that person to her and we could talk about it.

I immediately knew who I would ask, my insurance man William Theopple. I drove out to see him, and he agreed to make time to do this. About a

A Full Life or Life of a Fool

week later, he and I returned to Catherine's house. Within an hour we had an agreement to do just as she had suggested.

I was young and very "green" about buying a farm, and yet I did not want to seem too easy. When she said that she wanted $32,000 for the 120-acre farm that had 80 plus tillable acres, I quickly replied that I would be willing to give her $31,000. She replied in a very stern way, "No, I want $32,000." I quickly said, "Okay!" I was thankful that she did not throw both of us out of her house. Within a couple of weeks, the papers were drawn up by Ross McGuiness, a local attorney, and we both signed and that was it. Catherine scheduled a sale of all her farm equipment and some of her house furnishings for late September. I turned in my resignation at the dairy much to the shock of Mr. Cooper. We prepared to move in early October of 1962. I had only worked for the dairy for two years. Mr. Cooper stated to me that I might want to continue to work for him because he did not think I could afford to buy a farm and raise a family in those tough times. I thanked him for the opportunity that he had given me and was shortly gone from both Dallastown and the first real job that I had ever had.

My dad signed a loan for $5,000 at the bank that previously would not loan me anything, so I could get started farming. I hoped to buy some of Mrs. Reherd's farm equipment at her public sale. Dad also gave me an old plow that he had when he started farming. I bought an M Farmall tractor at the sale and all the tobacco laths. There was a tobacco shed about a quarter of a mile up the road which belonged to the farm. I thought I would raise tobacco to give me something to do in the winter months which is when the tobacco was stripped off the stalks and sold. I also bid on a corner cupboard that Dee wanted; however, the attorney who had prepared our agreement bid it up against me because it was an antique. I had to offer a huge price and this prevented me from buying some more machinery.

We finally settled in at our new farm. I bought some chickens (so we could sell eggs), a couple of hogs, and six young steers. I bought the hay and straw that was in the barn and some corn in the cribs at the sale, so I had something to feed the livestock. I now realized the truth of what Mr. Cooper had tried to tell me about how it would be tough to make it on a farm with a wife, two kids, and putting food on the table. So I got a job driving a school bus for the local school district. Soon after that, I was approached by the guy who picked up my eggs to take over his job. He lived down in Maryland and had egg routes that took a lot of his time. He was hauling eggs two days a week from Pennsylvania from 12 different stops. He wanted to pay me so much an hour and supply me with a truck to haul the eggs to his garage in Maryland which was 15 miles from my farm. The eggs all came from my area within a five-mile radius with me being in the center. He said it would take me about 12 hours per week, and I knew he was spending at least 16 hours doing the job because he always stood around and talked when he picked up my eggs. The farmers involved were my dad, six of our close neighbors, and other locals whom I knew fairly well. I convinced this guy to give me $40 a week to do this job. I worked it out with the farmers so that I could pick up the eggs very early in the morning, still having time to drive the school bus. After my bus route, I would take the load of eggs down to Maryland. This really worked out well and enabled me to put food on our table for several years. Finally, this guy could not stand to pay me that easy money, so he took back the egg route for himself. I quit raising chickens around the same time my father did because there was very little money to be made in the egg business.

Our two children, Kimberly and Bryan on our farm in 1965.

That first year on my farm (1963), I knew that I had to pay Mrs. Reherd both $1000 on the principle and 5% interest on the balance, which was $1600.

I would give her two checks so as to make things easy for bookkeeping purposes. One day as I was taking the checks to her house the day before the payment was due, she asked me why I was giving her two checks. I explained to her my reasoning. She calmly handed me back the $1000 check and told me to keep it. I told her no because that was hers and was the principle. She replied in a very firm and resolute voice, "You only wanted to pay me $31,000, and that is what I am going to charge you. You keep that because you might need it. I thanked her and probably with tears of joy in my eyes drove home to tell Dee. The second year that I paid Mrs. Reherd I only owed her $29,000. I knew that I had bought my farm at a good time and for a good price because land values were going up very quickly.

My fertilizer dealer Charles Trout and myself. This was a photo used by Olin Matherson Company; record PA potato yield: 860 bushels per acre.

After selling me her farm, Mrs. Reherd bought a big house in New Park which was about halfway between the farm she had sold me and where I grew up on our farm. My dad was still farming that land, and to this day, my family owns this land. Mrs. Reherd invited us to visit her with our kids, and we became very friendly, always enjoying the time spent at her house. That first year that I farmed, I invited her to come over and look at my potatoes while we were harvesting them; she did and seemed to enjoy that.

Being serious about this farming business and raising potatoes for the potato chip company, I decided to now build a hog farrowing house. I could raise pigs from birth until they reached 40 pounds and then sell them. When I went to the bank to ask for a loan, they told me they could not give me one because the farm was still in Catherine Reherd's name, and they would have no security. The manager, however, said they would loan me the money by allowing me $50,000 for a farm mortgage, plus a little more if needed. I talked with Mrs. Reherd, and she said that she was fine with me paying her off and moving it to the bank. I did that in the spring of 1966, and by that summer when it was so dry, I was even able to buy an irrigation system to water my crops.

Just a side note about that dry year of 1966 in York County, Pennsylvania. It affected many things such as the forests and trees as well as the crops. By 1990, when trees were being harvested in York County, the rings on the stump of one large old oak tree showed a noticeable difference. The ring for 1966 was of a width 50% less than the other rings. The rings of trees do not lie, and they hold that history for the life of the tree.

While I was building the hog house, I decided to weld the farrowing pins for the sows (mother pigs) area, and fabricate them myself with pipe that I was able to buy from John Novac, a guy from Lancaster County. This guy, who later proved to be a dishonest businessman, was in charge of getting rid of the surplus building supplies from the Peach Bottom Atomic Power Plant being built on the Susquehanna River which flows between York and Lancaster counties. This guy let me get one load of pipe on my dad's truck.

Then he told me he could not get any more pipe just yet because they were doing some blasting for construction. I soon learned that I might not get any more pipe because he had not been paid. I thought he would figure out something, and he did. He stopped at the farm and told me he had a tractor trailer load coming out of Maine in a few days. If I wanted the pipe, he would just deliver it to me and that would be enough pipe to finish my job. I told him ok, and he asked me for a check for $2500 which is what I was to pay for the pipe at Peach Bottom. My wise and cautious wife questioned the wisdom of giving this guy a check for that much money. My reply was that he had trusted me till now, and I needed to trust him. I later learned that he never had any intention of delivering that pipe and that he was a very skilled crook who had taken advantage of people all over this area, especially in Lancaster County.

Some weeks later, I became desperate to keep building my hog pens, but I still had no pipe and could not afford to buy any new pipe. So I got a friend to take me to John Novac's house one night. I scared him into giving me a check for the $2500 that he owed me. He thought I had a gun in my heavy winter coat, but it was only my hand and finger. Only his guilt and imagination completely convinced him that he would be better off giving me that check. I told him that the first thing I better see when he came out of the little office where he told me he kept his checkbook, was the check in his hand and nothing else. I further told him that he could wind up in the river the next morning if he tried anything. I left with the check in my hand, and as I attempted to cash the check, I soon found out that it was written against an already closed bank account. I turned the no-good check over to a local attorney, who fooled around with it for almost two years and got nowhere. I finally got all of my paperwork returned to me since he could not do anything for me.

Sometimes attorneys work too slowly. And in this case, I could see why. The two-year statute of limitations was going to run out in two more days. I jumped into my car and drove across the river. I went to the District Attorney's office in Lancaster, and as he looked at the paperwork he said to me, "This guy you are working with is a professional crook. But I notice something different, and this is really a crime because he gave you a check from a bank account that has already been closed, and in Pennsylvania, that is a crime." The DA said that this guy would not normally do that because he would just beat you out of whatever you were working on without giving you a check. He asked me if I had $35 with me, and I stated that I did. He sent me to an attorney down the street who filled out papers and charged me $35. I took those papers to an old black magistrate who lived near this John Novac. When he looked at the paperwork from the attorney he said, "My, My!" The deputy who was standing nearby said, "What you got?" The magistrate said, "This is for John Novac, and it is criminal." The deputy said to give it to him 'cause he just saw John go into a nearby restaurant. By 2 P.M., John was in the Lancaster jailhouse. Several weeks later, I went to a hearing in Lancaster at the magistrate's office. John's attorney tried to convince the judge that I made him give me the check at gunpoint. He had a fancy attorney, but I was just a young innocent guy that got screwed by a professional crook who lost the case this time. I got paid $1200 in cash and a note that will never be worth the time of day. I came out of it not too badly, but I learned how to be careful in a handshake business deal. There was a great deal of pleasure in knowing that this crook went down this time, and I just got wiser in the ways of the world.

I found several farms to rent for cash as a lot of farmers were quitting, getting older, or just wanted out of the farming business. That left me farming several hundred more acres of ground. Things were moving very fast, and I started raising more potatoes. In 1968, I was credited with raising the highest yield of potatoes in the state of Pennsylvania as measured by the York County Farm Agent. In 1969, the Gearing Corporation was giving away a brand new two row Lockwood potato planter to the farmer in Pennsylvania with the highest yield of potatoes. I was fortunate enough to win this prize with more than 860 bushels to the acre yield. I believe that record may still stand today as not many potatoes are raised in Pennsylvania any more. I would not have won that contest had I not been irrigating my potatoes.

I worked very hard and had good success even during 1966 when my neighbors' cornfields were only yielding 17 bushels to an acre, and my corn was yielding over 90 bushels to an acre due to my irrigation system because I had a big stream flowing through part of my farm.

One time I had tickets to an evening doubleheader baseball game between the Yankees and the Orioles at Memorial Stadium in Baltimore before it was called Camden Yards. I wanted to go to the game so badly. So I worked it out, but I never went to bed from Wednesday morning until Sunday morning when I returned home from the game. I slept right through Sunday breakfast, lunch, and woke up in time for supper. Then I went back to bed until Monday morning. I did not feel well for a long time after that, and I knew it was a very foolish thing to do. I did manage a few cat naps, lying down in the field along the edge of the cornfield shielded a bit from the sun and sometimes in the shade of a tractor wheel—but never in bed.

I stayed active in the York County Potato Growers Association for as many years as I grew potatoes. The years of farming tend to run together now as I search to write the highlights. It was a very busy time in our lives. My family and I attended church at several area churches over the years. My two children attended public school at first and then went to a private Christian school. Our son is now the principal of that school and his wife is the director of the kindergarten as well as a teacher. Their daughter is a teacher and coach there, too.

New Life 9:

Community Problems

In the 1960s in the area of Pennsylvania where I lived, country people looked out for one another. Some might even say it was clannish. The fact of the matter was that if something was not good for the community, all of a sudden, things would happen in order to get matters back in tow (that word meant that if it was out of line, it needed to get back in line). One such incident that deserved to be addressed was a very out-of-control family that was not paying their landlord any rent money. This was driving the community, the Pennsylvania State Police, and many other local residents crazy with anger; some were even scared to death, and some grossly affected by the actions of some of the brothers of this family. I guess they could have been called rednecks, and probably most of the residents in this community as well as myself could have been called rednecks.

One day as I was baling some alfalfa hay, I noticed there was a thunderstorm coming in from the West, which is usually where they began. My neighbor pulled into my field and started to help me bail hay and load it the wagon behind his tractor. As the storm grew nearer, we both finished the job and put the wagons in the shed. I asked him what I owed him, and he just laughed and said to ask his hired man why they were there to help.

This hired man and another man loading the wagons were guys that I had gone to school with, and one was even a close neighbor. They explained to me that they had been bailing wheat straw on a farm that they rented several miles to the east. Someone had come out to the field with a rifle and stopped them, threatened them if they did not leave immediately, and said he would shoot all of them. Not knowing what else to do, they pulled out of the field and headed home. They were driving past me and could tell it was going to rain, so they just stopped and helped me finish up my bailing. Remember there were no cell phones at that time.

The conversation continued while the rain came down. We were in where it was dry and satisfied the day's work was done. I had heard about this family and the trouble they were causing for our neighbors. I was basically the new kid on the block because of only living in the community for six years. I listened intently to the issues and became increasingly concerned that these human beings could be so corrupt as to do these evil deeds.

One night they had forced an elderly man, living alone in his trailer, to vacate the premises. They took over his home for the night, drinking and raising Cain. In the morning, after they told the old guy he could come back to his trailer, they told him if he ever reported this to the police that they would come back and kill him. The state police would only go the house where these bad guys lived in pairs because of the threatening nature of this family.

Several months before as these guys were driving totally drunk, they had crossed a yellow line on a curve in Maryland and caused an accident. This was just about five miles to the south, and we lived within a mile of the Mason-Dixon Line. This head-on accident resulted in the deaths of two young women. At that time, being drunk and causing an accident did not receive as severe a punishment as it does today. It was reported that these guys did not have any insurance and, seemingly, nothing was being done about this. Just a week before these guys threatened to shoot the men bailing straw, as if that was not enough, these brothers had set up a road block trying to rape a woman that lived nearby. She escaped by driving over some big limbs and got through the blockade they had placed in the road.

One of the guys who had helped me bale that rainy day knew the lady who was the landowner of the property where this rough family lived. He shared some more disturbing information with us. This lady had a fourteen-year-old daughter, and had lost her husband to a heart attack about a year earlier. When

A Full Life or Life of a Fool

she drove back to the old farmhouse to where this family was living to ask about why no rent was being paid, she was confronted with the following from one of the brothers. "We know your husband died, and we know that you have a young daughter. If you want to mess with us, then we will mess with you and your daughter. Just go away, and let us be."

This woman had just told this to my friend Charlie. He said, "We need to do something about this." I agreed, and later the next week, Charlie, my younger brother (who had recently been discharged from the Marine Corps and was back from Vietnam), and I, decided to check out what could be done to remove them from our community. We had to walk about two and a half miles across country to get to where they lived so as not to be seen by anyone. Yes, we were armed, but not dangerous to anyone else as we were on a mission to improve the community by ridding it of what seemed to us to be a very dangerous, deteriorating situation.

As we approached the house from a nearby cornfield with the stalks hovering more than six feet tall, we noticed a lot of people sitting around a table in what appeared to be the kitchen. They were drinking, cussing, and just raising hell. I crawled from the field into the yard in order to get a better look, while cradling my 32 spec.

Winchester in my arms. I was scouting the place out and it was pitch dark. I crawled into a guy just lying in the yard passed out and most likely drunk. I hear footsteps and realized that another guy was walking across the yard from the head of the rut-filled long lane which made it impassable with a normal car. I had left my brother and friend in the cornfield some 30 yards away. The house was about 15–20 yards from where I was ready for anything that would come my way. This guy nearly stepped on me, and I was ready to fix him up with my rifle butt. He did not even hesitate as he walked on by me and the passed out guy to my right. I took note that the cellar doors were off the entrance to the basement, and that would make easy access to the lower part of the house if needed. On my way back to the field, I noticed a sign that had been driven in on a stake into their yard which stated, "If you are not out of here in 20 days, all hell will break loose. Signed, the McClures."

The McClure family mostly consisted of a bunch of rough rednecks, but other than being just a bit rowdy, were basically good people. They would never bother anyone, if anyone did not bother them. In our community, that was all most people desired. It was good to know that someone else besides us was after this bunch. We tried to buy some dynamite from an old farmer because the lady who owned their house said to just get rid of the house, and then they would most likely leave. She had told Charlie that she did not care what we did to the house because it was not really fit for anyone to live in it. The idea at that time was to catch them away from the house and get rid of it while they were gone. But that plan failed because we could not find any fuses to use with the dynamite that we had.

Along came plan B with another walking trip. When we arrived at the house, we shot out the fuse box on the back porch which killed all the electric, so we hoped that would take care of the problem. It did not, so a third walk was planned. We took along much ammunition in order to convince them to leave by shooting high into the house and making them realize that the McClures or someone wanted them gone. After several shots into their roof, we started getting return shots from most likely a .22 rifle. Some of the bullets zinged off of stones not far from where we were. We realized that this could get ugly, and we had used up all of our ammunition in a hurry and got out of there. The next day, two of the brothers showed up at the house of the owner whom they had previously threatened. They told her they were leaving because someone was after them.

This was followed by the house being burned down just one day later. I never knew who did that. This family was never heard from again, as far as I know, from anyone in our community. Rumor had it that they moved back to the Carolina's. Many folks were much relieved that they were finally gone. Was it a good thing that we did? We knew that three guys and our community were relieved when they were gone. We, of course, never got thanked for what happened, nor did we ask for any praise. We just kept quiet and much of the community never even knew what had happened and our part in all of that.

Charlie was one of my best friends who had worked for a certain neighbor for many years since he had been a little boy, in fact. This farmer was like a dad to him. He told Charlie that if he wanted to build a house, he could have any spot on the farm. The time had come for Charlie to do just that as the tenant house that he and his family lived in was getting pretty well gone.

When Charlie asked for the piece of ground that he and his wife wanted for their house, he was told, "Not there, but any place else." It seemed that his boss wanted to build a house for himself on that very same spot. This so

A Full Life or Life of a Fool

angered Charlie that he quit his job. I asked Charlie if he wanted to work with me and told him we could share machinery. He could rent some ground and start farming for himself. We both agreed to do that, and we continued to do that until the day I stopped farming and Charlie continued to farm.

A couple of years before this happened to Charlie, his boss sort of took me under his wing. He wanted to finance a combine for me because I was about to buy a large John Deere 6600 combine. I had started doing some custom work as well as my own work. This neighbor told me to buy the bigger 7700 combine, and he would let me do all of his combining and also finance the combine. Being young and full of energy, this sounded like a good idea. So I canceled the 6600 and ordered the 7700. I told the John Deere dealer that I did not need financing as I had a person who was going to back me. My seemingly generous neighbor told me to let him know about a week before we had to settle for the combine. When the time came, I called my neighbor, and he wanted me to go to the Production Credit office with him the next day. He would pick me up at 9 A.M. I was familiar with this office even though I had not done any business with them thus far, but I had thought about doing so in the future. It was a good place for farmers to borrow money at less interest than the open bank market.

While we were there, a great big man who was very close friends with my neighbor, told me that based on his experience that I would not make it in agriculture. He suggested to me that I should sell out to my neighbor and work for him. This immediately bristled me, and I jumped out of my chair and called him a fat, no good son of a bitch and for my neighbor to get me home. I walked out of the office, but just before I left, I turned and told that man the following: "In about two or three years I will return with my financial records, and I will dare you not to loan money to me, or I will see to it that you are fired!" I banged the door shut and waited for my neighbor to give me the last ride ever in his car. It was a very quiet trip home, and my neighbor said that he guessed I would have to take care of my own financing. At that time, even though I was not sure what I would do, I was not putting up with any of that crap. That was about all I said during the 40-minute ride to my farm.

That fat man retired before the three years were up, but I went back to that same office in just three years as I had promised I would do. I had no trouble borrowing money at a good interest rate from that day until near the end of my farming career. I forgave my neighbor for what he did, but I did not forget the lessons in life that that experience had taught me. I had to eat crow though as I went back to the John Deere dealer and had to do a refinance on the 7700 combine. I got through it okay, but that was not a nice situation.

New Life 10:

Starting a New Business Along with Farming

Charlie continued to work with me and was also farming some ground on his own. One of the farms was the same property where the house had burned down. I did not realize this, but there was another old house some 1000 yards from the burned down structure. Charlie had been back there doing some work and believed that someone was living in that old structure, which was overgrown by briers, trees, and honeysuckle vines, obscuring it from view. Charlie asked me to go with him to check it out and to bring a gun, but I chose not to bring one. So one evening near dark as the day's work was finished, he and I went to this place. Sure enough, there was a hidden house. Charlie had brought his shotgun with him, and as we went into the old house we saw a door leading to the upstairs. It had been blocked or held shut from the inside. Charlie banged on the upper floor and yelled that if someone did not come down in 10 seconds, he was going to shoot up through the floor.

I was shocked as we heard footsteps overhead, and down came five young people. One girl and four guys who looked to be in their late teens or early 20s appeared. When Charlie asked them for identification, the one guy who seemed to be the spokesman for the group told Charlie, "We do not have to show you nothing!" Suddenly, Charlie discharged the shotgun, and this guy screamed, "You shot me; you shot me!" Quickly the identification started to flow. I was not sure if Charlie had really shot him or not, as all I had seen was fire flying out of the barrel of the gun in the darkness of all the overhanging brush. It turned out that Charlie had shot into the ground, and bits of stone had flown up and hit the leader of this group of young people who had claimed this house as their home.

The leader had long hair hanging nearly to his waist and wore an ax in a holster on his hip. The girl was from Baltimore, Maryland, and two of the fellows also came from there. The other guy was the son of an Episcopalian priest from somewhere in North Carolina. The leader was a local guy, the son of a nearby neighbor who had died several years before. His uncle lived across the field about a mile away. We marched them out into the open field and made them sit on the ground as Charlie and I discussed what we should do. At that time, I had a young guy working for me who was living in one of the houses on a property that I was buying. This guy was big and burly. He had just found out where we were and approached us and our discussion.

What we did not know at the time was that this band of five had been burglarizing the local high school for food from the cafeteria. An investigation had been ongoing. We told the girl and the three not-local guys that they had one hour to gather all their stuff from the house that they could carry. They were further told to leave and never look back unless they wanted to be buried in a plot down over the hill which already housed people like them from years ago. We decided to take the local guy to his uncle and try to get him some help.

During the next week, we heard reports of people seeing the four heading south toward Baltimore, and we never heard from them again. This guy's aunt and uncle told us that this guy was no good, and they could not help him. They had their own family and did not want to help this nephew who was out of control. They said they were sorry; we understood, but now we have a new problem. This guy whose name was Bob, explained to us what they had been doing and how they were surviving with the food they had stolen from the high school. I personally felt compassion for him and was thankful that Charlie had not shot him. Charlie was very upset with the whole situation.

Bob said that he could not find work and tried to excuse his condition. The four of us discussed his situation for several hours. I agreed to put Bob to work by the hour. I gave him a place to stay with big, burly Dan. I explained to Bob that he would have to live under my and Dan's rules. As of that minute,

A Full Life or Life of a Fool

there was to be no more drugs, no beer, no smoking. Nothing but work and clean living were to be his goals. I told him that first thing in the morning we would go to the barbershop in Stewartstown and get his hair cut. As I waited for him to return, he still had his hair at shoulder length. I sent him back to the barbershop with more money. When he came out again, I was going to send him back once more, but he quickly said that Mr. Lytle the barber said he now looked like a fine young man. So I eased up and back to the farm we went.

It was no easy task to get Bob to conform to farm work. I believe he wanted to do well, but so many drugs had made it hard for him to make the switch. Big, burly Dan was a great help because he was like a strict jail warden. But finally he eased up as Bob began to take hold. By the end of potato season, I told Bob that he needed to go and look for a real job. He found a good job at a plastic mold factory about eight miles up the road.

Bob worked there for years, and my wife and I went to his wedding later on in his life. He would often stop to occasionally thank me for saving his life. He told me that more than once, he had spent hours thinking about taking his own life before the evening of his rescue. This is a story that should remind us all, that sometimes, given a chance in life, things can work out for the good.

Charlie and I continued to work hard, and then another person came into my life who I would say was the best earthly friend that I ever had. Buck, as we called him, had quit farming, but he rented his potato storage to me. His children attended a private school in Maryland, and he encouraged us to try it for our two children. We did, and it was a very positive thing for our family. In fact, our son is now the principal of that institution.

Because of my years in the military and personal belief in God, I have always equated a true friend as one who would lay down his life for me, even if it would cost him his life. Buck was such a man. I have had many say they were my friend, or that I was their friend, but a true friend is really someone special. I believe having a true friend is an amazing thing.

Potatoes, which was our main crop, became very work intensive. However, some big changes were coming in our area to that business. Labor to harvest the crop caused the potato harvester to replace the older way of harvesting potatoes; it was faster and less labor intensive. A neighbor and I decided to buy such a potato harvester and wound up starting a business together. During the next few years, we sold more potato harvesters to fellow farmers in our area than any other existing business.

The potato industry now had seven potato chip factories in our area. Many potatoes had been grown here from the early '40s to the '70s. I can remember my father telling us at the supper table one evening in the early '50s, that during his two trips to Hanover and the UTZ potato chip plant that day, he had observed a newfangled thermometer that was going to spell trouble for us farmers.

The truth was that it was a hydrometer. By weighing out eight pounds of raw peeled potatoes and floating them in water, they could test the specific gravity of those potatoes. This meant that the higher the specific gravity of the potato, the more pounds of finished chips each 100 pounds of raw potatoes could make. This could vary as much as eight extra pounds out of 100 pounds of raw potatoes.

Several years later it became common knowledge that the higher the elevation where the potato was raised, the higher the specific gravity would be in that potato. Thus, potatoes raised at a higher elevation were more than worth the extra freight that it cost to send them to those seven potato chip factories. Because York County, PA, is only about 800 feet above sea level, this became one of the primary reasons for the decline in the potato industry here.

Thus, at the Wilson farm the primary focus of raising potatoes turned more into a grain intensive farming operation. The tire, battery, and oil business which was started in the early '70s, had grown rapidly. I had bought out my partner and was looking for a place to move my tire business seeing as how all my farm buildings were now full of tires. So in 1978, I bought a large service center several miles up the road above Stewartstown. I began to move the business on the farm to that location. The farming operation continued to grow even as the two began to separate. For a long time, some of the employees of the farm worked at both places as needed.

During the fast growth of the tire business, I crossed paths with a large tire recapping facility about 50 miles from my shop. I was paid 80 cents per tire to remove about 40,000 tires from that facility. I built a place to house these tires so that I could resell them for farm implement tires. These tires had been rejected for recapping by a large cross-country trucking operation. However, they were fine to use on slow-moving farm vehicles such as large manure spreaders. I was able to sell those casings, as I got orders for them, at $15–$20 each. This was a very profitable business. When the local township found this out, they were very jealous of my success and came after me in a zoning battle that lasted for many years. I fought it, spending very little money.

A Full Life or Life of a Fool

On the other hand, the local township spent thousands of dollars trying to prove that I had done something wrong.

At one time after bringing 21 criminal charges against me, they had to drop those charges. Then they brought 9 civil charges against me, charging me with more than a million dollars in fines. During that process, I was forced to take all of my records from my tire business to the office of the attorney who was working for the township. I had gone to school with this attorney, and there was no love lost between us. This attorney was very well-known as someone who was making a lot of money off of zoning rules, and he was somewhat of an expert at bragging that he was the local expert. I detested his attitude, and at every turn did not make it easy for him. I did not trust him as well as not liking what he was doing to other people who were resisting the rules he was trying to establish in the local municipalities.

When forced by the judge to take my records to his office, I bought two gallons of the most potent disinfectant that I could find from a fellow hog farmer, and I soaked the records with it. When I arrived at his office, wearing my permitted .45 caliber pistol, his secretaries screamed that I had a gun. It was holstered, and I did not threaten anyone with it. The attorney assured his people that I was not a dangerous man and asked me if I had the records with me. I told him that they were in my truck, but he would have to carry them in and back out if he wanted to see them. So he did, and as soon as they were in his office, the whole building began to smell strongly of the disinfectant. Shortly, the upstairs was evacuated of all those office spaces, and the owner of the building was called. There were nine boxes of records and they were put in the main office. Meanwhile, I was putting only small amounts of change into the parking meter so that I could step out and get some fresh air from time to time. I had also soaked an old pair of shoes in the disinfectant and scraped it on everything and everywhere that I could in that office.

By noon time, only one secretary remained in the attorney's office. He told me I would have to leave because they were closing for lunch. I told the attorney that he would have to load those records back on my truck. He called the judge at the courthouse, and the judge asked me what was on the records. I told him how the mail used to be disinfected for different reasons. I did not trust this attorney, and I did not want anyone to sue me for making someone sick with these records, so I had bought disinfectant and applied it to the records. The judge told the attorney that he would have to deal with it. I finally let him off the hook for carrying them to my truck during lunch after he called my attorney, and my attorney talked to me. So the attorney sent me to a place for lunch and called a York policeman, in the meantime, who accosted me on the street, pushed me up against a building, and told me that he wanted my weapon off me right then and there. I explained that I had permission to carry it. I told him why I was there, and I also reminded him that I knew his chief as I used to be his milkman. I told him that I would call his chief and have him fired for harassing me. He admitted to me that the attorney had called him. But then he told me of a closer and better place to eat lunch. I went there only to find the lone secretary who was still working in the building where my records were. The only seat open was at the bar where she was sitting. I sat down beside her, and she asked me what that terrible odor was on those records.

I asked her if she knew anything about farming. She told me that she had grown up in York, but now lived out in the country by Dover. I explained to her about swine and how I kept my records in the hog house which was probably a little too close to the boar pen. I reminded her that when an old boar hog gets excited, he secretes a kind of smelly stuff that is really needed to breed the sows. At that point, she stopped eating, got up and left. I did not see her when I got back to the attorney's office, so she must have gone home. As I spent several hours in the office with the attorney, and before he carried the boxes back to my truck, I made numerous calls on his phone system. I tried to worry him about how much it might cost him to have me in his office. I had a bunch of futures in the market, and I was really just checking every few minutes on the prices using an 800 number. But I do not think that he knew what I was doing.

As the attorney finished his work, he needed to make a dozen or so copies. His copier was not working, so he called across the street to the firm where he used to work and asked to use their copier. As he crossed the street, an attorney in that firm who knew me well, saw me following this attorney with my .45 strapped to my hip. Later, he told me that he went into his own office and lay on the floor and laughed and laughed because he knew what was going on!

In the end, it went to trial, and I was found guilty and charged $1. The only other money that I had spent was for gas and the disinfectant. I was ordered to move the tires by the end of February, I did not appeal, but I was forced to get rid of many tires which I could have sold in the next several years for a large sum of money.

New Life 11:

Selling My Dream

During the late 1970s, after purchasing the service center and the Massey Ferguson dealership north of Stewartstown, I more than doubled the square footage of that facility by building an addition. We eventually dropped Massey and put in a full auto parts store. We named that business the Wilson Service Center and remained as such until 2015. I still own that facility, but I have sold it to a former employee.

As I had promised the manager of the Farm Credit or Production Credit office in York, I returned with my financial records and started borrowing money from that institution at a very low interest rate. Interest from my local bank had risen by several percent, but I had no problem borrowing because my equity had increased greatly. It was hard to keep the records exactly straight because I was mixing money that I borrowed from the local bank and from Production Credit. I had over a million dollars borrowed at that time, and as the interest bill grew, I was having trouble making enough money on the farm to pay all that interest. My interest bill by 1980–1981 was more than a thousand dollars a day, and that was seven days a week, and we only worked six days.

Our children were growing up, and I was always worried that because we always had money that they might grow up without having a sense that money did not grow on trees. Around 1975, my wife and I started giving our two children an allowance in return for all the chores and work that they were doing. We told them they would have to buy their school clothing and pay for their entertainment out of that allowance. We took vacations to Atlantic Beach, North Carolina, during the summers. They would each decide how much money to take so that they still had money left for school clothing. We paid their dental, doctor, and food needs, but we let them take care of the rest.

Both of our children told us in later years that this had been a very good thing for them because it taught them the value of money. Another lesson that I passed on to them was that if being in business was your job, then there was a responsibility to be available to the public at all times. Often I would have to discuss something with an employee, customer, or someone in the community during meal times at our house, so I had a long phone cord installed near the table for this purpose.

The interest burden had gotten so high by 1981 that I felt in order to preserve my ability to do what I wanted to do, I would sell the farming operation. I would rather have sold the service center, but the high commercial interest would not cause anyone to want that responsibility. On the other hand, farming with low interest was still very popular, and the competition to rent ground was great. Knowing that I had about 2000 acres rented and owned another 450 acres, I made the decision to sell my farming operation. I then built a large house on a three-acre lot on the home farm, and by the end of 1982 we moved into a new, large stone home. We sold the farming operation one farm at a time during the next four years to a large operation from Maryland. Next, because I felt there would be too many chiefs and not enough Indians at the service center, I decided to take a job as a sales representative and sell farm equipment. My heart was still in agriculture, and that was what I wanted to do. My son who was by this time in college but home for the summer, pretty much built our house along with some help from Charlie and a few other folks. I had a horseshoe court built in the basement with a 13-foot clearance so the shoes would not hit the bottom floor of the house. At the time, I was pitching horseshoes as a professional, and I really took the game seriously. Both of my children pitched, and that was quality time that we would spend together. Only my wife did not care for the sport, but she always cooperated with us as we would travel some distance to different tournaments on the weekends. The basement of that house became a recreational hot spot in the community, as it also contained a regulation size ping pong table, shuffleboard court, dart board area, a place to ride bicycles, and a golf driving net. A lot of fun times were had there as community groups and high school groups could gather there in the winter months as well.

I had always been my own boss since I left the Marines and my milkman job and started farming in 1962. But now I was going to work for someone else at another business known as Penn Jersey. This was a big change for me, but I loved it. I was traveling out to farms and selling large silos and big manure tanks to mostly dairy farmers.

After several years, my brother-in-law decided to leave the service center, and as he had been the lead guy there, I had to resign my job and go back to the service center. I put in a computer system so we could track inventory more easily, and we transitioned into a new way of doing things. By now, my daughter and my sister were doing the books at the business. The owner of Penn Jersey would stop in at the center every few months and still ask me if I would come back to work for him. I really wanted to do this, seeing as how I had a good son-in-law, good parts man, and was able to rehire my good brother-in-law. I decided to make those guys partners in the business and take myself back to Penn Jersey.

By 1986, I was going through a big fight with the IRS. They claimed that I owed them $90,000 because they ruled that I had not sold my farms one each year, but had sold them instead all at one time. We fought them, but as we did, we found out that my CPA firm had not filed a timely appeal. So that was why they were coming down on me so hard. I had to go to Congressman Goodling's office for help. Now he had been my guidance counselor when I attended Kennard Dale High School and had forced me back then to take the new courses offered to prepare me for college.

Congressman Goodling assigned a very smart lady to my case, and she found out that the CPA firm had erred. They had actually created a fake timely appeal and sent it to the IRS to try to cover their tracks. I had to go to the Federal Post Office building in Philadelphia to the IRS office with my accountant who had committed this fraud that was never discovered by the IRS. I wore a bug (tape recorder belonging to my attorney) inside the pocket of my undershirt as advised by my attorney. I was to discuss the fraud not in front of the IRS officer but with my attorney on the way down and back from Philadelphia so we could use that evidence if things did not go well for me.

The first thing that happened as I went through the first metal detector, which I had not seen, the alarm went off, so I had to go back out and re-enter. I was smart enough to know what the problem was. I quickly said that I had an emergency bathroom call and must get there fast. They escorted me to a bathroom on the outside of security, and I removed the bug and placed it in the trashcan. I got through the metal detector now with no problem. I could not tell my accountant what had happened to the tape recorder. We went up several floors to the IRS office and discussed and argued with the two IRS agents for over an hour. At the end, we made an agreement that the IRS would accept a check from me that day for eighteen thousand dollars, and they would remove the liens that they had placed on my bank accounts within 48 hours, and all would be well. Going back downstairs to where we had entered, I told my accountant that I did not feel well and wanted to go back into the bathroom for a bit. I told him to wait for me because I would not be in there too long. I recovered the tape recorder from the trash can, put it back inside my undershirt, and we went home. My CPA firm could have lost their license and been fined for what they had done, so they were more than willing to make it right with me as they continued to do my accounting for several years until I finally left them.

Thinking all was well and that the liens were gone, I got a call from my bank several days later saying that the IRS had removed all the money out of my account again which they had already done several times. I was extremely upset and called the IRS office. I spoke to one of the agents that I had talked to when I was there who had struck the deal to remove those liens. I told him that if they did not put that money back in my account immediately that there was going to be blood shed! He told me someone would come down from the Lancaster IRS office to calm me down. He warned me that I could not threaten the IRS. I told them they had better bring an army because I would fight to the death for my rights. He pretty much knew that I was pissed.

I hung up the phone, and several minutes later he called me back and said the Lancaster agent had erred, and the problem would be straightened out immediately. He again said that someone would be down from the Lancaster office. I told him again that he better bring an army. I was both angry and determined to stand my ground.

I drove home and got my .45 caliber pistol and my 30-06 deer rifle and returned with them to the service center. I told all my employees to leave immediately if the IRS should come, and I would take care of the situation. I also called the local TV station and told them briefly what happened and that I did not intend to shoot anyone, but I would hold them hostage until this mess was fixed. I gave my address and phone number. Then I just waited for someone to come.

No one came. About two hours later, I got a phone call from my bank. The same man who always called to tell me about the IRS taking money out of my account said, "Mr. Wilson, I cannot believe what just happened. All the money that the IRS took out of your account has been replaced. I have never seen this happen before." I believe that it probably was just a mistake, and I am glad that it worked out the way it did. That was actually the last bad experience that I have ever had with the IRS.

By 1995 the business for whom I was working had some tough times. Milk prices were low and changes in the industry caused the big blue silos, as we called them, to be in less demand. The dairy farmers had resorted to large trenches and big loaders in order to feed the now larger herds of dairy animals. Three of the salesmen, including myself, were let go, so I just retired.

Soon after retirement, I became involved with the local school district from which I had graduated. I was elected to the board of directors and served for eight years, with four of those as president. In 2002, I went on a trip with the German class as a chaperon, and my granddaughter who was a senior student was on that trip. We toured four countries and had a great time.

It was a very good experience for I learned much serving on that board. My worst fear was sitting in on hearings with students and parents of children who were being disciplined. I had not always been a good student, and I feared I would have great difficulty in handing down the proper discipline. To my great surprise, the recommendations made by the principal and superintendent in all the cases was very reasonable. It made my job a lot easier than I had expected. I had to help negotiate several contracts for teachers. The teachers' union would fight for their rights as expected, and the board would try to be fair to both teachers and the taxpayers. I learned a lot from the teachers and from Tracy Shank who was the superintendent for most of the time when I was on the board. I always tried to put an end to politics in our school system which was a very hard thing to do. Politics should have nothing to do with the proper education of children, but often times it got in the way of good employees trying to do the right thing for the students.

I also spent ten or more years on a private school board before serving on the public school board. While both were trying to teach children life skills, discipline, and how to live together in society successfully, there was often a much different outcome. While some would blame the teachers for their children's failure to grow up properly, my experience was that if parents did not do their job right, it was only by the grace of God, that some good teacher had a good influence on that child to guide them on a right path. In the end, it is up to the individual as to how they face life. In America more than anywhere else, a person can choose how he wants to live.

By the time I came home from that trip to Europe, I got a call from Marvin Zimmerman who was a builder of the silos that I had once sold. He asked me to meet him at the York Fair as he had an exhibit there. He was now building and also selling used silos. He had an opportunity to buy a franchise to sell the same equipment as Penn Jersey. Marvin told me that he knew nothing about selling or getting the government forms filled out to assist the farmers who wanted to buy manure tanks. He asked me if I could help him start the selling part of his business. He was already doing the repair work, but he wanted to expand his operation. This equipment was made in England and then shipped to the USA ready to build. The equipment was exactly the same as what I had sold at Penn Jersey. A.O. Smith in Chicago had built that plant in England and eventually sold it to a company called Fusion. The ten years of no competition had now passed, and they could export to the USA. I agreed to drive up to Oakland Mills, Pennsylvania, that next week to view the operation. While I was there he instructed me to draw up a contract to do all of his selling. I did, and he signed it. So now I am no longer retired but back in the grind of selling equipment. I would be selling against the same company for whom I used to work, but I found that as a challenge and really enjoyed the work. My territory was the entire East coast from Maine to Florida as well as the area east of the Mississippi River. During the years that I worked for Marvin, I put nearly 100,000 miles on my car each year. I always picked up a new car every year as I did not want any problems while out on the road. The car of my choice was a red Oldsmobile Intrigue. I sold many structures and made Marvin so busy that his business experienced growing pains which made it soon hard for him to manage. Many businesses experience those kinds of problems especially finding good help. After four or five years, Marvin asked me to redo my contract. Even though I could have done that and made plenty of money, I declined. Instead, I once again retired.

A Full Life or Life of a Fool

While I was farming, there were two people to whom I must refer in my book. I considered both of them to be a very important part of my life. One was an International farm equipment owner, and the other was a mill and general store owner. When I began farming in the '60s, I bought feed for my livestock and chickens, and some farm machinery from Charles Manifold. He and I became business friends and sometimes he would share advice with me. It was very evident that he cared about me. As time went on when I built the new hog operation, he explained to me that I would need some credit for things that I had to buy. He told me that he would carry my needs from month to month and not charge me any interest. He also told me if he could be reached by phone, that meant that he was in town. He would get me anything I needed even if it was after hours as he knew that I was working long hours to try to succeed with my business. On many occasions, I took advantage of that offer and was able to work into the night because I could get the right part for a broken piece of farm equipment from him. His business was located two and half miles from my farm in the village of New Park, PA. As time went on, interest began to creep up. Mr. Manifold explained to me that he was hurting a bit financially as he was now borrowing money to keep his business going. He would need to start charging me interest. Respecting his wishes, I paid my account down as quickly as possible both to cooperate and to spare myself of the extra burden that had been thrust on me by the interest charges on my bill. This was completely justified. I knew that Charles had also trusted other young farmers to fulfill their obligations to him, but some did not. I hated that because he was a good man. In a few years, I had paid off all that I owed him. I have nothing but good memories of this kind man. On one occasion, I used Mr. Manifold as a credit reference. For some reason, I got to read his recommendation.

Where the word "honesty" was to be rated, he gave me a 99%. As I looked at it, I thought he was saying that I had not been 100% honest with him. Since I could talk to him about anything, I simply asked him if in some way I had shortchanged him. He laughed and told me that no human being is 100% honest, and we both had a big laugh.

Mr. Keiser was the other man who had a wonderful influence on my life. As I mentioned earlier in my book, he and his wife ran a general store, post office, mill for grinding feed, trucking business, as well as selling coal, fertilizer, and seeds. I enjoyed many fun-filled days with their two boys, hunting big bull frogs in the mill race. By the time I started farming, those kids were all married and gone, but the businesses remained. In the mid or late '70s the post office was closed by the US government. I started buying fertilizer from Jim senior in the mid-'70s. We became close business friends, as I bought many seeds from him and spent a great deal of time discussing farming. Much the same as Mr. Manifold, Mr. Keiser took an interest in me and my farming operation. He extended credit to me which really helped me to get from planting to harvest. He would haul grain for me, and as he and I were both buying grain futures, we would compare notes as to what we thought about the markets. As my operation grew and I had several tractors and trailers, he got me started buying certified grain from Freemont, Ohio. He set me up hauling asphalt shingles on my way West and then hauling grain on the way back east. Near the age of 60 while hauling grain to Virginia, Jim was fatally injured in a truck accident. He gave up his life to save hitting a car with children in it. During the next few years, his widow carried a heavy burden. When that accident happened, the market turned down. The margin calls on his contracts went unsatisfied for several weeks. I was privy to that information because I also had margin calls to which I needed to attend. Jim and I had just talked about this the day before his accident.

To make a long sad story shorter, Jim's wife, Mamie, called me. She asked if I could help her sell some property that they had acquired from a farmer who had not paid his bills and instead have given them some land. My wife and I met with her on a Sunday afternoon and tried to help her through her pain. She managed to sell some property, but it took ten years for that estate to be settled. It left her with nothing but the store and a few acres. She had a nice pension from the post office, but she wound up moving into a rented apartment.

One of the things that I did while helping Mamie was to help her son Jimmy who had become somewhat ill. He was going through a messy divorce and was trying to keep his farm. He was dealing with the same bank from which I was borrowing money. I met with Jimmy, whom I had not seen for years. He explained to me that he had not missed a payment, but they sent him a notice stating that the bank was taking his farm. The bank stated that he had a ten-year loan with a balloon payment, and the balloon was up. They were closing him out. I got Jimmy to write a letter which I took to the bank and talked with the bank president, the loan officer, and the bank attorney. The bank could not find the bank file on the loan, and I suspected something was wrong. I could tell the attorney for the bank did not feel comfortable with

A Full Life or Life of a Fool

the situation. I told Jimmy he had to find the loan papers. After much searching, which had been very difficult for him, as he struggled with ill health including diabetes taking its toll on his eyesight, he found the papers. Sure enough, it was a 20-year loan, and he was paying over 13% interest.

Instead of calling the bank, I called Washington, D.C., and they transferred me to the Pennsylvania State Banking Commission. About two hours later, I got a call from the bank president, and he asked me why I had made that call. He told me that it could cause the bank big problems with a full investigation. I simply stated to him that I believed that is what should happen, and it was a shortened conversation.

The next day after sleeping on all that had happened. I decided to call the bank president to whom I had spoken yesterday. I was told that he could not speak to me because he was in a meeting. I told the receptionist that she had better get him on the phone immediately. She asked me what this was about. I told her that the president was most likely talking to the attorney and the loan officer. She replied, "How did you know that?" I told her to just tell the president who was on the phone and all would be well. She did, and several seconds later, I was on the phone with the president. I told him that we had found the missing part of the file. The loan was for 20 years, and he promised a call back later in the day to give me more information. He called back and told me that the bank would rewrite the loan for 10 years and reduce the interest to 7%. The bank followed through, and Jimmy got the matter resolved.

While checking further into the situation, I found out that the bank officer had been having an affair with Jimmy's previous wife. She had asked him to close out the loan so she could get the bonds that were being held as security from the messy divorce. I know that bank officer was removed from the bank, but I am not sure what happened to him after that. There is much more history between our family and the Keiser family. I was just glad that I could be there for Mamie and her children when I was needed.

Mamie continued to confide in me, and I tried to help her as much as I could to ease the pain of the loss of her husband any my good friend. Until she died about 20 years later, we remained in close contact. She even asked me to be her executor. I would later do her storing for her and pay her bills. When she finally went to a convalescent home, I learned a valuable lesson in life. When a person is an executor and not the one who has power of attorney, he cannot help the person for whom he has to manage their care. After several discussions with her children, I was also assigned the task of power of attorney and continued to watch over her until her death.

During those years, she taught me much history of Muddy Creek Forks and many stories of how Freddie Grove had helped her through many situations in the store. Mamie was a very attractive lady who always kept herself looking nice. She was always friendly to everyone who came into the store, but some men took advantage of her nice personality. She told me she would beg Freddie to stay at the store to basically protect her from some of those men who would always come in if they knew Jim was out on the road doing his trucking. She said that Freddie never said anything inappropriate to her except for one day when he said referring to her figure, "So round, so firm, and so fully packed!" I guess that was Freddie's way of complimenting Mamie.

Mamie never wanted anyone to know her age. She would reply to anyone who asked her, "Age is a number and mine is unlisted!" She warned me later on that if I permitted her birth date to be placed on her tombstone, she would come back and haunt me. I made sure that I carried out her wishes. All of that was a small price to pay to Jim and Mamie for all that they had done for my wife and me.

New Life 12:

Finding Out Why I Was Me

Dee's mother and father were in a bad car accident on the way home from Lancaster County one day. Her mother, Meda, passed away, and in 1984, her dad, Leroy, passed away as well as her sister's husband, Elmer Keeney.

Our son Bryan was coming back from finishing college in South Carolina with his wife in order to live here in this area. He had prepared to be a teacher and was looking for a job. His wife, Dreama, started working for a real estate firm in Shrewsbury. Bryan was helping at the service center redoing the parts department, and we were putting in a computer to modernize things a bit. By the time Bryan got his full-time teaching position, he had the service center looking beautiful.

After the trouble with the IRS, I hired on my son-in-law Bill Johnson, Ken Webb, and my brother-in-law Jack Wolfe. Then I went back to working for Penn Jersey. I was also playing a lot of golf and loving life as we were living in our new stone house. Those years seemed to have gone by rather quickly, and now grandchildren were here and others on the way.

In 2004, my brother, two sisters, and I drew up a partnership for our mom and dad. They gave us all of their possessions to take care of for them as they were nearing their 90s. Dad had fallen several times, and the big farmhouse with all the floors and stairs was too much for Mom and Dad to take care of now. We called that partnership RGRG (Richard, Glenda, Ronald, Gloria) Partners named for the four of us siblings, and it is still alive and well today. We agreed that we could not spend any money on ourselves as long as Mom or Dad was still alive. Mom is 100+ at this time. This is something that families who get along well with one another could implement today. Sad to say that seems to be a problem in today's world.

We bought a new condo in Stewartstown for Mom and Dad. Dad wound up in a rest home and did some rehab for a time, but he eventually made it back home. When Dad went to the home after being in the hospital, his Medicare payments were soon to run out, and he would now be charged by the day for his stay there. Dad told me that he wanted to be out of there, so I promised him that I would try to accomplish that. I went to the nurse's station and asked what the procedure was to get him out of there. The nurse told me that I would need to speak to the director, and he was busy in a meeting.

She tried to discourage me from removing Dad, and I told her that I wanted to do it legally if I could. I waited at the door of the meeting room for about 45 minutes. When he came out, someone had already told him why I was waiting there. He explained that he wanted my father to stay there for at least one more week. I reminded him that it would cost a lot of extra money for Dad to do that, and Dad really wanted to go home. He argued with me a bit, and as I was warming up to the conversation, I stopped him and told him I wanted to ask him a few questions.

I asked him if he understood farming, and he said that he did. I told him that a chicken can only lay one egg a day, and he said he understood that. I then told him that if you had a chicken visiting your hen house and that chicken laid three or four eggs a day, the desire would be to keep that chicken and not want it to leave. He said, "Okay." Then I told him that my dad was not going to be his chicken. His response was," I will get your dad out of here this afternoon." He did and all went well.

About a year later, Dad passed away in that same rest home. I was with him when he died. I knew he had been suffering, and I had just had a long talk with him. I assured him that we kids would take care of Mom, and if he was ready to go, not to worry about anything here. About 15 minutes later as I sat alongside Dad's bed, the nurse said to me that Dad was about to leave us. Two minutes later, he passed into eternity. It seems to me now, that it is really important

A Full Life or Life of a Fool

in a situation where you have a loved one hanging onto life, to make them feel as comfortable as possible and assure them of your help to take care of things once they are gone. I have thought a lot about that after that particular night.

I was still playing a lot of golf after 1990. On my birthday in 1995, I was 55 years old and shot a 72 at the Pleasant Valley Golf Course. My USGA handicap went to a four! That was the lowest it had ever been, but it has climbed much since then. I still love the game because I think it is played on green grass, and that is my favorite color. The group with whom I played, took a lot of trips, and I had much fun playing that sport which had replaced my horseshoe playing.

I had always promised that someday, I would I take my mom and dad on a trip West to see their relatives before they got too old to do that. Dee and I finally decided that the time had come for that adventure. We carefully planned the trip. I had a nice big Chevy Impala with plenty of room for our luggage. I was in between retirements at the time, so we did not have many obligations. Away we went. Another purpose of the trip was to see some of my customers by traveling through Maryland and West Virginia. I wanted my dad to be able to talk to a couple of my customers to whom I had sold equipment. I was proud of the fact that I was not a high pressure salesman. My customers respected me and were, and always would be, glad to see me come to their farms. They welcomed my family, and we enjoyed several conversations with these former customers.

As we rolled westward, we went through Robert Dole's hometown of Russel, Kansas. One funny sight was an old Chevy car mounted up high near the center of town that had been the town police car many years ago. Dad always liked hearing Mr. Dole say, "I know it; you know it; and we all know it." Getting back on the main highway heading west, I was driving about 70–75 miles per hour. I saw a car gaining on me rather quickly, and as he passed me, by dad said, laughingly, "I wonder how fast that guy is traveling." I hit the gas and caught up with him for a bit. He was doing about 115 miles per hour, and so was I. I slowed down as my wife and my mother were somewhat frightened. My dad said, "That was the fastest I have ever gone in my life!" He was chuckling as he said it. We could see a mountain far ahead of us that turned out to be Pikes Peak in Colorado. That evening we ate in a Spanish restaurant in Colorado. As my dad was about to order, he asked the waitress how the Spanish oysters were because he loved oysters. Now I knew we were a long way from water.

She told my dad that they were good if you liked them. I told her that she had better explain to my dad what they were. When she told him they were bull testicles, Dad quickly replied, "Damn if I want that," and we all laughed.

Later on that evening, we called one of the cousins who lived in Colorado who was the son of dad's brother. His wife answered and told us that three of the brothers were camping somewhere out on a piece of ground southwest of where we were. It seemed that they had bought an 8N Ford tractor and were preparing to build a camp or some small house on that property. I asked her to give us directions, and she was not very encouraging. I wrote down what she said. The next morning at 6 A.M., we left the motel and went to search for them. We had to leave the main highway and travel several miles off of any road to get to where they were. They were staying in a tent. Sure enough, there was the 8N Ford tractor and down over the hill was their tent. When we pulled up to the tractor, the three cousins in their underpants rolled out of the tent thinking that we were stealing the tractor. They were dumbfounded to find their cousin and his wife with their aunt and uncle whom they had not seen for a long time. After they got dressed, they rode into town with us and we enjoyed breakfast with them. Next we were on our way to see some more relatives who lived in Utah.

The plan was to go to Mexico in order to see Mom's oldest brother, Kenneth Dellinger, and then stop in Phoenix, Arizona, to visit Donald, Dad's only brother. They had not seen one another for quite a few years and that would prove to be the last time they would all be together alive on this earth. So this proved to be a very timely trip for us to take. Little did I know that this trip would have a very big impact on my life as well.

Entering Mexico at the border, we went through Tijuana down to Ensenada. We stayed there one night and proceeded to my cousin's place the next morning. There were my uncle Kenneth, Aunt Gertrude, Cousin Donna, and her husband, Herb. My Aunt Gertrude was in the late stages of Alzheimer's, but she appeared to be happy. Uncle Ken was nearly blind but still able to get around. Donna and Herb were making the best of it, enjoying the beautiful sunsets every evening as they were on the beach. Next, we were back to the USA and Arizona.

We met at Donald and Bonnie's house in Scottsdale, Arizona. Soon we were joined by other relatives. My Uncle Walter Bartol, with whom we had visited in 1960 on our way home from the Philippines, had long since passed

A Full Life or Life of a Fool

away. Now I was to meet his son, Walter Bartol Jr. Everyone called him "Junior." I really took to him and wanted to talk with him to quiz him about his father. As fate would have it, my wife and I were to go home with Junior and his wife to Peoria which was part of Phoenix. Dad and Mom were going to be with Junior's sister and her husband somewhere in downtown Phoenix. We were going to be taken on a big trip the next day to the Roosevelt Dam high up in the mountains. That is where the water came from which was used to irrigate the land around Phoenix. My wish had come true, and I was going to ask Junior lots of questions about his dad whom I had grown to adore just in the small amount of time that I had spent with him those many years ago.

Junior was now retired and owned much of the land around Phoenix which they were farming. We spent several days with him, and he showed us many interesting things, including a farm that raised and sold rose bushes. Junior had recently worked for a bank and had amassed a big portfolio of small farm owners of whom he was very proud. None of them had ever been a problem to the bank. But now they were trying to force Walter to stop loaning money to these smaller farm owners because of many other banks that were merging with bigger banks. Junior just up and quit because this practice angered him, saying that this was a sign of the times.

Junior hired several vans in order take all of our family members up to the Roosevelt Dam. One of the reasons he did that was to be able to tell us about his dad who had come west, worked at a livery stable, and then fought in World War I. When he came back to Phoenix, he bought that same livery stable during the time when the dam was being built. The United States government planned a trip for the then-President Roosevelt and vice president to travel to the site of the dam. The government approached Walter to haul the vice president up to the dam from Phoenix. On the way up, they stayed overnight in a building that was still standing as we drove up the winding roads to the dam. President Roosevelt was to be taken up by a car for the christening of the dam.

As we made our way up this narrow road, we could look straight down to thousands of feet below. There were no guardrails, and we could also see remains of vehicles that had not made it safely up or down this road. My dad and his brother talked the entire way up and down. It was really good to see those brothers enjoy the last few days they would spend together on this earth. I, in turn, spent a great deal of time talking with my second cousin Helen, who was Junior's sister. I asked her a lot of questions, and she told me to get Junior to sit down with me and tell me more about his dad. She could tell that I was very interested. For the next two days, Junior and I talked, and I began to realize something very important. It was not because I had been born backwards that caused all the stuff that had happened to me in my life, nor was it the way I felt about certain things, nor the way I reacted to certain things, nor some of the crazy things that I had done. It was because of my heritage. I could now see in my Uncle Walter a very clear picture of myself!

Walter Bartol in uniform, World War 1.

Junior told me that when his dad was making money and doing "his thing" in his younger years, he would take a young couple under his wing and help them get started in life. If they did well, and paid him back whatever he loaned them, and heeded his directions, then he was happy and would sing their praises. He also had said that if he tried to help someone out and they tried to take advantage of him, he would be the most ruthless SOB that they would ever know.

A Full Life or Life of a Fool

He told me of one time about a guy who needed a horse when Walter was running the livery stable. His dad let him have the horse on credit, and the guy promised that the next time he was in town, he would pay for it. Several years later, this guy was in town and still had not paid for the horse. In fact, he was in a bar bragging about how he had gotten this free horse from Walter. Walter found out where this guy was and sent someone over to the bar to fetch him. When the guy showed up at the livery stable, Walter shot and killed him. The new sheriff that had just been hired in Phoenix, went to see Walter, and explained to him that he could not do that kind of thing anymore. Phoenix was just changing to a new system of law and order. This true story is on tape in the library in Phoenix as part of the Heritage of Phoenix.

As Junior told me other stories, it was very easy to see what made me tick. I did not try to be like I was; it just came out. That was a wonderful trip for me, and I value all that I learned about my favorite great uncle. It should also be known that he was the only great uncle that I had ever met on the Bartol side of the family. Uncle Walter, in my mind, was the only person that I knew who influenced me without me ever knowing why until this trip out west with Dee and my parents.

The big stone house that we had built and lived in on Draco Road was now too much for Dee to manage. She could not do the basement stairs, so we bought a condo very close to the one that RGRG had bought for my mom and dad. After I was no longer on the school board, I was elected to the board of the homeowner's association that took care of running the 132 condo units at Bailey Springs. I was still traveling a lot with my job and would sometimes be gone for several days, but because of cell phones coming into existence it was easy to stay in touch with Dee.

My mom continued to live in the unit just two streets down from us, and soon my brother and his wife bought a condo on the next street down from us. However, there was a problem with the organization that had built the condos where we all lived. I was then appointed to head up a lawsuit that had been filed shortly before I became a member of the board. The lawsuit simply stated that there were deficiencies in the construction of the condos that would later cause problems for the owners of the condos.

I pledged, after being elected to the office of president of the condo association, that I would remain as such until this lawsuit was settled. Twelve years later, it is still not completely settled. However, our association had been given money by the court system, which has helped to keep the association healthy and not in debt to fix the problems that definitely had caused expenses in the past years. I hope to be relieved soon of my position, as I think the end of the lawsuits are about to occur.

I then had an opportunity to go on a golf trip to Florida in February. I went with several of my golfing friends to a house in Weston, Florida, which is located near Miami. The nine of us would stay for several weeks and play golf every day. The weather was nice and warm and reminded me of the Philippines which I had dearly loved. After quite a few years of taking this golf vacation, I realized that the owner of the house would eventually not allow us to stay there. So as the winter of 2010 arrived, I told Dee that I might try to buy a place in Florida when I next traveled there. I looked at several places but decided not to buy one until the next year. Dee asked me why I was doing this. My reply was that I knew I wanted to continue to go to Florida during the winter months to play golf and that is what I thought I should do. Property rates were lower than they had been when I first went down to Florida years ago. I found what I thought was the right place for us, bought it, and sent back pictures to Dee. When I returned near the end of February, Dee said that she would enjoy going down and looking at what I had bought. I asked her when she wanted to go. She said not before next week, and so we left on Monday.

Dee thought the place was a good buy, but a lot of the furnishings that came with the place were old. They could be replaced with newer items. We quickly did some minor repairs. Now every winter since then, in October we head down to Florida until the Thanksgiving holiday, and after the Christmas holiday we go back down until near springtime. We drove down for several years and took along enough clothing and items to keep there, so that now we can fly and not have to take any luggage. That works out great for us. We have a car in Florida and a car in Pennsylvania. I travel back and forth about five or six times a year, but Dee just makes the two annual trips.

In 2014, I accepted the job of governor in my building in Florida. I was elected president of the 432 condo association units. So much unbelievable stuff has happened there that it would take another book to explain all of it. I may or may not write that second book, but this one is about finished. On a more pleasant note, my dear mother Erma is now 100+ years with a sharp mind, living in a convalescent home of her choice. My brother and sisters and I visit her nearly every day.

A Full Life or Life of a Fool

Back in the early 2000s, I had a major stroke that damaged my eyesight; fortunately, it did not paralyze me or affect my speech. A few years later, I had another stroke, but it was a transient ischemic attack (TIA) which just messed up my life for several hours. Then another major stroke a few years later, followed by another TIA a year later. After my visit with the neurologist, he told me they could find no reason for my having a stroke because I had better than normal readings on my blood pressure, cholesterol, heart rate, and had no curated arteries. I was a bit overweight, but they could find nothing else. He said they could have had me swallow a camera and taken pictures inside, but by the time that was done, I would most likely have known little more than I now knew. I asked him what my chances were of having more strokes. He said, "Pretty good." However, he further stated that I might live to be 95 years of age and die from something else. We agreed that I would just go on in my normal routine and see what would come my way. So that is what I am doing now. I love and appreciate life one day at a time. I have lived a full life, and I know to some, it may be the life of a fool!